**Other titles by Patrick Summers**

*Key Change:*
*An Alternative History of Mozart*

*A Collection of Brevities*

*The Spirit of This Place:*
*How Music Illuminates the Human Spirit*

# THE PRISON OF TIME

Poems from 2023
Patrick Summers

Contenti Press

Copyright © 2024 Patrick Summers

All rights reserved. No part of this book may be used or reproduced in any manner without written permission from the author, except for brief quotations for critical articles and reviews.

ISBN 979-8-9876023-5-5

Design by Pattima Singhalaka.

*Dedicated to the memory of
my late brother, Philip Anthony
Summers (1942–1996).*

*He was known to his Indiana family
as Tony and to his chosen California
family and friends as Phil.*

*He was poetry in our lives for
the short term of his.*

# CONTENTS

Long Poems ................................................................................ 1
On Melbury Road, London ..................................................... 2
A Puzzlement ............................................................................ 3
Late Night on West 82nd Street ............................................. 5
Aspen 2022 ................................................................................ 9
Auditions ................................................................................. 13
The Last Night of the 1970s ................................................. 19
Balmoral .................................................................................. 23
Beau Revoir ............................................................................. 26
Bike Accident in Melbourne ................................................ 32
People I Must Avoid .............................................................. 36
Labor Day, Cincinnati, 1978 ................................................ 37
His Eyes ................................................................................... 39
Leaving Sydney Opera House ............................................. 40
Legacies of Great Art ............................................................. 41
Cost .......................................................................................... 43
Covent Garden ....................................................................... 44
A Reminder of Cruelty .......................................................... 45
Cy Twombly Gallery, Houston ............................................ 46
Dark ......................................................................................... 47
Trusting No One .................................................................... 49
Summer Storm, Washington, D.C. ..................................... 51
Santa Barbara ......................................................................... 55
Emily Knwarreye .................................................................... 57
Epiphany in Central Park ..................................................... 58
Fireflies .................................................................................... 62
Flaws ........................................................................................ 66

| | |
|---|---|
| Fort Worth, March 2023 | 68 |
| Dear One | 71 |
| We are Not as Funny as We Used to Be | 74 |
| Geist | 75 |
| Adolf Hitler | 76 |
| Jackie | 79 |
| Katy Trail, Dallas | 81 |
| Knowing | 84 |
| Krakatoa | 86 |
| Ruining the World | 87 |
| Lost Brothers | 89 |
| Mansefeldt, August 2022 | 91 |
| Mark Wagner | 95 |
| Mauthausen | 97 |
| Millennial | 99 |
| Montmartre Déjà | 101 |
| Murmurations | 103 |
| Near Dover Hill | 105 |
| October Questions | 109 |
| Old Women | 111 |
| One Truth | 115 |
| Polmood Dawn | 116 |
| Paraclete | 120 |
| Lucienne Boyer Sings "Parlez-moi d'amor" | 126 |
| Pat Robertson's Heaven | 129 |
| Photo of Our Parents, November 22, 1941 | 131 |
| Phra Alack | 133 |

| | |
|---|---|
| Playing House | 137 |
| Playing in the Rain | 139 |
| Looking at Potsdam from the Train | 141 |
| Presence | 142 |
| Red Speedo | 145 |
| Standing on the San Andreas | 146 |
| Sausalito Summer, 1968 | 148 |
| Unfinished Symphony | 153 |
| The Line | 155 |
| Semele | 156 |
| Simple Elegy | 157 |
| Time | 158 |
| A Toilet in Berlin | 159 |
| Trost | 162 |
| Vienna Moment | 164 |
| Walking in Kensington Gardens | 166 |
| On Waterloo Bridge | 169 |
| Winter Trees | 171 |
| Thirty-Six One-Word Poems That Happen Each Day | 173 |
| Wreckers | 176 |
| Hearing the Brahms Second Symphony for the First Time | 178 |
| United Methodist Church, Washington, Indiana, 1979 | 180 |
| Nilo Cruz in Aspen | 182 |
| Strasbourg Cathedral, 2001 | 184 |
| Thoughts During *Das Lied von der Erde* | 186 |
| Patty, Sally, Phyllis | 190 |
| Chipmunk | 193 |

First World Problem ................................................................ 196
Carrying the Mountains Home.............................................. 197
New York City, Autumn 2022 .................................................. 203
Marfa ........................................................................................... 206
Untitled (dawn to dusk)............................................................ 208
Swimming Under the Blue Moon............................................ 209
Sunset in China ......................................................................... 211
September ................................................................................. 213
A Poem for Lynn Wyatt ............................................................ 216
The Prison of Time.................................................................... 221

# Long Poems

I have noticed
That my prose poems
Are all long.

And I know why:
Because sometimes
We notice that we
Love so deeply
That we do most of the loving.

# On Melbury Road, London

I spent many hours there
In what felt like my youth.
Guests of generous friends
Who lived on the little curving street.

It was, for me, pure London
Gracious huge Georgian houses.
Luxurious newness renovated.
Queen Victoria down the road
Ever-present in her mournful weeds.

I've seen Melbury Road at every time of day.
Jet lag often had me awake so I would
Go outside and walk the curve, dipping away
From Holland Park. Often lights would come on.
What had other nights seen on this beautiful road?

Benjamin Britten, coming home from *Peter Grimes*.
Carriages galore, I'm sure, at all times of day.
London must have been very noisy then.
Clop. Clop. Without end.

It was the place of dreams.
It still visits mine, often.

# A Puzzlement
## Matthew Walters Young
## 1967–2022

We attempt in vain to understand.
We read about Hephaestus
Or Vulcan or Loge, the old ones
Called upon to explain fire.

But none of them go far
In revealing our dear friend.
What happened to him?
When did he lose touch
With the little boy we all knew?

Tasked with misunderstanding,
We look for what we thought we did.
Or what we did not do.
I knew him well when he was a teen.
I was with him when he turned twenty,
And almost never since.

He was one who had everything.
Looks, brains, ambition,
But he could not define himself,
Nor say what he wanted,
From life, from women, from men,
From himself, from the world.

For me he remained a child.
He carried an adult's weight,
Even as a child.

But he was no child.
Those who took his childhood joy
Should not be walking among us.

His body was filled with summer.
Tanned, dark, shirtless, happy, carefree.
His soul was winter, cold and wrapped.
He needed the elemental fires of the world.

How could he have ever reached
Such a place in his soul?
And how could anyone
Express the pain
Of his last dozen hours?
I cannot.

Ancient gods of fire were invoked
To explain their purposes:
The spontaneous blazes that come from
Volcanoes or other forces of the earth.
But those ancient deities cannot tell us
Anything about this beautiful young soul.
Did he just want to hear his mother's voice?

# Late Night on West 82nd Street

Walking a dog in Central Park,
Not my dog…long story,
But a wonderful doggie, a golden.
Beautiful, needy, sweet, epileptic.

Wet cold of winter.
Gloves and scarves.
Christmas decorations.
Distant carols from brass choirs from
The more famous part of the park.
Tired horses who would all
Rather be anywhere else.

In the park,
I let the dear golden off leash
So he could be a dog.
Always so joyful,
So energetic in the park,
Instead of being a big dog
Unable to move
In a little apartment
On 81st and Columbus.

Every morning and night,
We would play in the park.
But he liked the night the best.
We were almost always alone.

Walking back one night,

Especially wet and cold,
On 82nd Street,
Past the Beresford,
Where famous people
Emerged out of taxis.

Walking just a few stairways further,
On the ground I noticed a head shot,
An actor's photo, the one he used
To try to make it all work.
A lot was riding on that photo,
At least for a few months,
Perhaps earlier that year.

He was handsome and inviting.
In the instant of the photo,
He was eager and beautiful.
Happy, so full of promise.
The photo was wrapped in plastic,
It was a photo he paid a lot for.
Beautiful young dark eyes,
Eager and hopeful,
And his smile,
Contented and expectant,
Was now in the trash.

I picked him up,
His wet and warping photo.
This was the last possible time
Anyone would see him like this.
By the next morning
He would be carried away
And never seen again,
So I took him home with me

And the gorgeous golden.

There were a dozen letters
Hidden underneath the photo.
Written to him by Jenn.

"Nobody made me feel like you did, baby,"
One of them said. Then in another, she wrote,

"I love when you said you could
Fuck me every day for the rest of my life…
And if you could do that…
We could live forever…I love when
You said that, baby…you know how I
Loved it when you fucked me…"
She wrote like that, with all the dots.
She made some of the dots,
Above the "I"
Into little hearts.

There it sat, wise words:
"We could live forever"…he told her that.
That is why we all do it,
Why we all seek it forever and constantly,
No matter the dangers.
This is why we allow it to hurt us:
Fucking feels like living.
And we think that as long as
We keep fucking
We will not die.

Captured in the shutter's fraction,
This was a man who felt many orgasms,
And he would feel many more,

Somewhere out there in the country
But not in New York. His explosions in Manhattan were done.
He thought he loved each one.

Did he become an actor?
Was he throwing out his photo
And moving back to Duluth or Dallas?
How many dreams had to die
Before he threw out love letters
Along with his photo?
What happened to him?

Or had he been even meaner
And sent his love letters back to her,
And was she throwing them out
Along with his photo?
Trying to forget him would be so difficult.

I wanted the girl to feel better,
And I was suddenly mad
At the handsome boy.
He should have been nicer.

The golden was tired from
Our park exertions.
So he put his head on my lap
And went to sleep.

# Aspen 2022
## Last Day of the Aspen Music Festival
## Sunday, August 21, 2022

The mountains have witnessed everything.
They were here when Mozart died.
They were here when Shakespeare spoke his own words.
They were even here when *Stegosauruses* roared through the canyons
And drank from the roaring creeks.
A little snake was stuck in Scanlon Hall a few days ago,
   listening to Mozart.
I was the only one to see him, I think.
I didn't want the artists scared,
So I put him in a bag and took him outside.
Trapped in a place he could never imagine,
What did he hear? (Can snakes hear?)
Did he hear our tired restlessness and inspired exhaustion?
It was that special Aspen shift of light, midevening.
Unearthly beauty and cooling warmth,
Distant green-maroon hills,
When you can still see dinosaurs because
   they wander in and get lost.

There is a myth of normal that burdens us all.
Normal is simply each of us at our best,
Not scared,
Bettering,
Honesty without harm.
We tell stories of others, looking for ourselves.
Who has made their way into our memories?
The wonderful young artists look to us,

Waiting and full, hungry and empty.
They don't yet know that the work is *all* emptiness,
Because it takes years to feel, as deeply as you can, that
Emptiness is the fullness you must give away.

The one who broke you cannot fix you,
But the one who helps you will never break you.
We find our inarticulate hopes and stuttering thanks.
Peace is the only truly inside job. Help them seek it.

Mozart crackles with life.
He is an ember longing for air.
He flares and smokes, before calming back down,
Waiting for his next breath.
*Sentilo battere.*
Verdi occupies all space, filling the vibrating sky.
He leaves a vague fear of something not happening twice.

That young one in the funny shorts is quiet and cerebral,
Scared, often sad, on a bike heading home to think.
Overlooked for the moment, but not by everyone,
And not forever. Does he know that
Being an artist is not pretending all is good,
But seeing good in all, including his mirror?
Teaching is precious, wild, sacred, clutching an ancient fire
Of sacred, wild, and precious truths
That both nothing and everything are enough.
Giving to others and letting go are the same act.
What if we miss the moment?
What if they need us and we aren't there?
We trust they will find their way, and *that* is the truly sacred event.
They must accept art as freedom, not as a cage in search of a bird.
Brilliant colleagues teach me every day. Gratitude.

If you find yourself in need of remembrance,
Remember the golden Colorado morning light.
Remember the practicing trumpet by Castle Creek,
Repeating Haydn until he is inevitable and bubbly.
The Mendelssohn Nocturne—the beauty of blood and bone.
The cheeky fox that knows no fear as she stalks,
Protecting her red babies,
All longing and fierce energy.
Remember the fish jumping for their dinner in the early evening,
And the chill of the nights while the rest of the world baked.
Remember the Welshman, not singing or acting, but *being*.
All the world's a stage, some brilliant person once said,
And Sir Bryn lifted all of us towards it.
Refuse to be someone's chapter if they are your book.
Refuse to be an almost.
We must be like the mountain, which makes you work,
Then it tires you,
Then it offers you a view.
What goes home with me?
Whitaker Blue Rhapsody
Brightness of Light, O'Keefe and Fleming and Steglitz and Gilfrey
Poetry, Love, Stillness, Wonder, Peace.
Covid. Covid. Dull. Dull.
Pacifying Quartet; Dreams of a Midsummer.
Eight Encounters with Opera, feeling like eighty.
Double Brahms is never enough.
Loads of High Notes: Arie Vardi and Arias of Verdi
Falstaff trilling the whole world.
Verdi quickening all pulses.

Lights of recognition turning on. Is-this-my-life thoughts.
Happiness. Work.

The hills were alive, as they always are, with the sounds of music.
With comforting children, plus flags and a manufactroversy.
Rites of Spring are the Rites of Summer.
Lando landing; Prokofiev standing
Brownlee and Huang, hanging on each gorgeous note.
Ludwig Concerto, the sacred fourth, endless mountainous beauty singing through it.
Aspen sunsets are in G major.
Rach 2, as ever, rocked, too
New music from the ether of the young. New Anthems.
Wayfarer's Songs were the Will and the Way
Symphonies of New Worlds make new New Worlds.
Raining on Tchaik's violins; Mahler 5 reining it all in.
The great Don condemned again by his own chosen dinner.
Mozart and his dad.
Masses for the Dead, quickly making *Barely Ohs*.
His opium and vodka, insanity and brilliance, timpani chords.
A liminal space between here and wherever there is, but
It is what beauty means *here*, not there.
Autumn approaches. The aspen trees will get cold and go to sleep.

They have already yawned, just in the last few days.
Soon, wherever we are, we will hear *September Song*
(Is there a greater song when Ella sings it?)
Either forget everything now or never forget *anything*. Choose one.
Look back without staring.
It cannot be escaped: we fall in love with music every day.
Will the snake now ask the bemused fox,
Why is Monday so silent?

# Auditions

Decisions that deeply affect lives,
When you are on my side of an audition,
The judging side.

"Everything you do, you still audition,"
Stephen said, and he was right.
But still, with hundreds to hear,
You have to think about what is listened for.

There are so many, so much need.
Sometimes I will not listen
For more than a minute,
Which seems terribly unfair
But it is also the most fair.

If I listen longer,
It is because there is a sound,
A sonic personality,
A gleaming connection to a word,
Sometimes just one word,
Usually an Italian one,
And it glistens with meaning.
It is meaning we listen for.
Meaning we seek.

And one looks for love.
Love of music.
Love of one's voice.
Love of being alive.

They are all gifted with desire.
So much need. So much hope.
They worked hard to attain this moment.

So many notes that have to be sounded.
Composers labored over them for years.
Their voices reaching to their own gods,
Giving their voice to others' voices.

How many times must I write,
"Lacks distinction"?
What is distinctive?
How many of the notes must be out of tune
Before someone tells them?

How many times will they sing *how many times*?
"O quante volte" by Bellini,
An incomplete title meaning "how many times?"
How many times, what?
This is what: "How many times have I asked
And begged for your love?"
Can you please sing it so that it means that?
Does it have any meaning to you?
How many times will I hear that aria
Sung with no meaning except
"Please hear me."

The gorgeous *Faust* aria, from so many of the tenors.
Why can they not simply make it a love song?
Demure, chaste, pure, and divine?
Make it sound like what it sounds like, please!

And what of Violetta's perfect questions?
*Sarìa per me sventura un serio amore?*

*Che risolvi, o turbata anima mia?*
*E sdegnarla poss'io per l'aride follie del viver mio?*

So much music begging for purpose
And for alignment
With whom and what we are now.
Not only bringing the past alive,
But bringing the past forward
To speak to us again like it was yesterday.

What will they all do with their lives?
Only a few will sing for many more months.
The sensation of singing must feel wonderful.
But what about the heartbreak they will feel
If they do not receive a place in the art,
The place for which they have trained
And for which their parents
Have sacrificed everything?

Endless hours with teachers who
Rightly want their charges to feel good,
And who rightly praise their improvements,
As all teachers should.

Then, in almost a dozen out of hundreds
You hear the sound
Of a coming generation.
Someone who brings an idea fully formed
To the simplicity of a phrase,
And you suddenly hear it like it was new.

"The spirit of this place,"
Mozart's Susanna says, just before the gorgeous aria.
Mozart suddenly meets his newest voice,

And it overwhelms with beauty.

The voice is inside.
It comes from inside one person
And enters me.
The most personal and intimate thing.

The bowtie, the one in the bowtie.
He kept watching my reaction.
He had the am-I-good? look or
The please-think-I-am-good look.

Most of the auditioning singers are somehow
Connected, however distantly, to what the west
Used to call *Cathay*, a word we aren't now meant to use.
Ideas of expression that are different from the west,
More inward, often truer than
What often passes for acting.
*They*, as *we* so often refer to *them*,
Are the unquestioned future of *our* beloved art.

The American Century of opera has begun.
And the American Century is, like our country,
An immigrant art again, but not from Europe.
The Asian Century it will be, very soon, and very nicely.

A world of dreams opens to a great voice.
To that special moment when you hear
The sound that you know will capture what
No one else has ever captured.
The future of Mozart is in their throat.

Tremendous energy thrown at things
Over-singing beyond belief

While wondering why we don't think she's enough.

Sunken shoulders, leaning forward
Grabbing the womb and the body's core
Far from their voice, trying to find it.

Love me. Want me. Hire me.
Just, please *notice me.*

Why does anyone sing that awful bass aria from Bizet's
*The Good Woman of Perth*? Was she really so good?
And the entrance aria of Massenet's *Manon*?
Just, why? What are you telling us?

The sad ones trying to hold on to their youth.
Like the soprano going to great pains
To tell us she has a green card.
Desperate for any job
Because it will keep her life intact.

Each singer gives new hope
Some fall out from the beat,
Randomly placing notes wherever it suits.
Discipline is too confining,
But discipline is the only freedom.
Discipline isn't rules.
Discipline makes disciples.

So many Mimis from act one
Quite a few from act three
So few capture the unique text
And make her into a real person.
More often she is a singer rather a seamstress
Scared and ambitious instead of just being.

Francia, Italia, Grecia, Patria mia
A speedy flight we'll take.
In a world of old gods,
How we will speak to a world that has new ones?
*Io vivo quasi in ciel*, Alfredo sings in audition after
Audition after audition. *I live like I'm in heaven.*
So why doesn't it sound
Like a young man in love
And feeling like he is heaven?

*Ewig wäre sie dann mein*
Forever she will be mine.
*Dich, teure Halle grüss ich wieder*
Great hall, I greet you again.

These little quivering souls
Vibrating the air with their gifts
Looking to us for approbation
Wanting only for a moment
To look as beautiful as they sound
Or to feel as beautiful as they are.

# The Last Night of the 1970s Ballroom

We all have a night that never ends.
The happiest night of our young life.
New Year's Eve, 1979, Julius in the West Village
Farewell to a decade. The time of our lives.
My second year in New York City.

I had danced my way out of Dunkirk.
The one in western New York, not the famous war Dunkirk.
For my eighteenth birthday, in the big year, 1976
Mom and Dad wanted to do something special.

From twelve to eighteen,
Dad drove me three times a week to Buffalo.
Buffalo.
That's love.

Dad decided we all needed a break for
"The only bicentennial we will ever have."
And he drove us seven hours to New York City.
My dream was coming true.

The Royal Manhattan.
Not nearly so royal as its name.
Strange straining hallway noises.
Men with men, overheard.

Dad promised one show, all we could afford.
We saw *California Suite*, which I loved.
Then came his surprise. *A Chorus Line.*

The dream of every dancer.

I cried when he told us at 6:00
That we were seeing it at 8:00.
July 3, 1976, the night before the big night.
Was the best night of my whole life.

All I ever needed was the music and the mirror,
And the chance to dance for you.
That was my night of nights
Until the last night of the '70s.

Paul's scene arrived like a bomb.
The scene where Paul is discovered in drag
By his parents, and his dad calls him son.
For the first time.
I didn't know the scene was coming.
None of us did.

I should have cried, but I was too stunned.
Because my dad, the one who drove me to every lesson.
My dad, who brought us all to New York for this moment.
Was in tears, crying for his own son, who he knew would leave.
New York would take his only son, from that moment forward.
And my dad was crying. I had never seen him cry before.

It was the full force of love for me that night.
The sweetness and the sorrow.
The gift was ours to borrow.
Won't regret, can't forget.
Mom looked at me, knowing all.

Outside, late at night on the eve of the bicentennial.
My parents let me take a walk alone to take it all in.

Now, all of these years later, I realized that they
Wanted time together, just to be with each other.
It did not occur to me then. Teenagers are selfish.

We went home, but my heart never left NYC.
Within a year I was back, and suddenly I was me.
I was the one in front of Michael Bennett, auditioning.
I got a job he approved of, in *Best Little Whorehouse*,
While he was doing *Ballroom*. I had arrived.

Is this the stuff of poetry?
For me it was. Dreams were coming true.
The '70s came to an end as we danced.
We finished New Year's Eve,
The last night of the '70s,
After the show down at Julius.
Me and Michael and the *Ballroom* gays.

That was the night I met Grant.
Who finally took my virginity,
Though everyone assumed it had been Michael.
No, I saved myself for the one
Who made the waiting worthwhile.

We spent the first day of the '80s in bed together.
We could not stop. I did not want to stop.
The desire was like blood or protein or oxygen,
An insatiable epic primal need.
Lacking it would bring death.
I had to have him, again and again.

He was the only one who was ever inside me.
Which was not the story of most of us.
But only a few dozen months after we said farewell to the '70s,

Grant got a lesion. Within weeks, I had one larger than his.

Love and fidelity did not save us.
We were misinformed.
Grant was the first to die.
Leaving me to face my passing alone.

On the night I died, my mother played *Chorus Line*
On my record player. She seemed happy, somehow,
That I did not have to die in a hospital, like so many.
About an hour before it came to an end, I asked her

To play me the final song from *Ballroom*.
I was never sure if it was a dream or real.
But Michael came to my room to say good-bye.
He was there, I was sure, as we listened.

I wish you a waltz.
Some people never go dancing.
They don't hear the music of the band.
Some people never go dancing.
So how can they understand?

# Balmoral

The River Dee crackles; it does not roar.
It bubbles with life but never draws attention,
Such a strange river, more of a creek.
Who decides what is or is not a river?

Was Queen Victoria ever naked outside?
Surely at Balmoral it would have been safe.
The Dee crackles, filling all other sounds while
Being essentially soft in the air.
Birds ascend and approve, and the happiest
Rabbits on earth assert their own majesty.

Helicopters and so many cars send the rabbits
Scurrying like the deer.
The estate is a danger for them,
Especially on this day.

Living simply, even in a five-hundred-room castle
Is perhaps the grandest of metaphors.
And so is this: what are we to do with our birthrights?

Was it young Elizabeth's task to give away her inheritance?
Trust.
Holding *in trust* was her job
For her whole life, whether it be long or short.
It was a service she did not seek nor define.

The world has moved beyond monarchs, except:
Wherever we don't have them we make them up.
Armies must swear oaths to someone, not just an idea.
Countless hours of watching the public leave
Westminster Hall. One man lives with me still:
"I was a grenadier, and we bear her," he said,
His voice breaking with tears.

The Grenadiers, only eight of them out of thousands,
Eight in Scotland, a different eight in London,
Were the ones bearing her frail old body
In her dense coffin made of lead.

All of the Grenadiers held her, all of them bearing her.
They would bear her on coins and stamps, as did we all,
The most replicated image of all of history's women.

Kings' daughters are among thy honorable women,
Says the most gorgeous coronation anthem.
When God appointed earthly kings,
Questions remained unanswered, questions like,
"Why would heaven's King bother with a small island
On an obscure planet at the edge of an endless space?"
Would he not have much more to do?

The horses and the deer at Balmoral
All call the estate home.
Somehow they know that something is happening
On that day of the helicopters and many more cars
And all of the rushing and the calls and the sadnesses
Emerging from the stone manor.

The animals have no monarch but nature.
They never did. Survival is their Sovereign.
Can they be happy if they are surveilled their whole lives?

And long before Queens or Kings, there was the Dee.

# Beau Revoir

The end was in the beginning.
Each was in the other.
Love or obsession?
Thoughtful, good, kind, generous.
That was him.
That *is* him.

Wounded, too, from indifference.
Parents married to beliefs above all,
Emotional chasms,
All the youthful needs still screaming their wishes.
Children stuck as children.
Sad Peter Pans who miss what they never had.

Constraints, hedonism, duties,
Pleasures have been many,
Circling our mutual fascinations,
Planning our lives,
Bringing us to an end.

We all live two simultaneous lives:
Our life as it happens,
And the life we choose to remember,
The time we choose to have,
The time we decide to witness.
The time we take to deepen our deepest sense.

Those parts of us that cannot be translated.
Try to speak to us with tenderness.
Something in our love went silent in transit.

Living to the core, with the volume on full silence.

Borrowed time, yesterday passed.
Four Last Songs have played their last.
Neither wanted to part; neither could stay.
So much will remain unresolved play.

Our balloon was set adrift,
A small separation here,
A glance at someone there,
Not this television show,
Not that one distraction,
Just not this…
Not today…
Always, "not today."
What day if *not* today?

Intrusions.
Exclusions.
Embraces.
On the bridge in Jackson,
On Waterloo.
In Moscow, Zurich, Seville,
Madrid, Paris, always London.
Christmas in Wells,
The great Cathedral gleaming.
We were so happy.

In front of our friends,
Within nature's embrace.
The nature of time,
The model of beauty,
Stood everywhere.

The great witnessing mountains,
Loved ones from the world.
Out in the cosmos,
So beautiful from there,
Are there the needs and desires
That cause us so much anguish?
Do hearts break on Venus?

Where is my heart?
Can anyone explain to me not
*How* we fell out of love, but *why*?
We now say we "grew apart,"
For that feels easier.
We were born apart.
We grew together,
For a time.

If there is a life awaiting us after this one,
Will we meet again?
I felt a forever love the moment I saw him.
Where did it go?
This was what *forever* must feel like.

When our souls lift from
Wherever they are now,
(Is my soul in my mind?
No one can tell me.)
Will he miss me then?

We are built to be answerable.
Is the rest *really* silence?
Where did my boy go?
He went here:
The science books start with questions,

But Bibles start with certainty.
He thought he was certain.

A persistent illusion.
Becalmed for resolution.
The strangest funeral
For what is still living but gone.

No cause. No cause.
Is the world so arbitrary?
Is there a creator?
(His mother would hate me for asking).

If yes, *who* created this awful heartache?
If no, why do we do this to ourselves?
We look into the deep past for answers.
Consciousness is the monarch that rules all.
But it lies to us with such glee.

Waking me one morning,
Sober as one could be,
He said, calmly,
"My mother is dead."
Suddenly, my own mother was resurrected.
I wrote obituaries for both of them.

This created world that was us
Was so beautiful for 144 months.
Well, we wanted it to be so.
The long list of those who loved us together,
They will quietly go on with their lives
And wonder what happened to the *us* they knew,
To the *us* that is gone.

Our yesterdays will live with us.
And longer than always,
Our little friends who didn't know our names
Will bring our love to the surface of their gentle minds.
Abby, George, Julius, Molly, Henry, Arthur.
Abby was Beau: ferocious energy
Not knowing where to burn.
George and Henry were me: *just love me*,
All need and obsession.

We tell our stories again and again,
Changing them,
Softening,
Caressing our wound,
Looking for a way out with grace.

There are no demons in our story.
Does it mean something that the
Sun is older than water?
Love is art, a higher insight.
Like any art, we can't know
How to do it until it fails.

We needn't believe in gods
If we believe in men.
We must weigh our actions
Against whatever avails itself
For our happiness.

Untune the string
That has been
Singing for so long.

Blow out your candle, Laura,
And each of us.
The taper has burned to its end.

# Bike Accident in Melbourne

Walking along the Yarra River.
The walk I did every day
In those beautiful halcyon Melbourne days
Of southern autumn 1994,
The months I had always called spring
Because up north everything is opposite.

Melbourne was new but familiar.
Almost like home but not home.
A place to start anew.
I loved it as I have loved few cities.
My loves are mountains, not buildings.

Walking home along the Yarra,
From CBD to Toorak,
From St. Kilda Road to Como Park.
I was listening to the first book
I ever bought on cassette,
A gorgeous book about dogs by
Elizabeth Marshall Thomas,
And I was loving the book,
Hearing it on my fat yellow
Walkman cassette player
That needed eight batteries
For its little life.

Far ahead of me, a cyclist was coming very fast.
I could sense another cyclist behind me.
Both of them were too fast.
The accident, though,

The moment that changed everything
Plays in my memory
In slow motion.

"Rounding your right!"
I heard from behind me.
They were traveling so quickly.
I figured since they drove on the left
I should walk on the left, too,
Since that is what everyone did.
I stepped off the path to avoid them.

The cyclist coming towards me did not slow,
Neither of them did.
They collided hard in a terrible crunch.
I can still hear them both moaning in pain.
My white T-shirt was covered in their blood.

The boy who had come from behind me
Went into convulsions, and his eye was sitting
On his cheek. His eyeglasses had shattered.
I had a jacket that I put over him, but I knew I had
To get an ambulance and get him to an emergency room.

I scrambled up an embankment.
Ran across Alexandra Avenue, dodging traffic.
I ran to a house and asked to use their phone.
"Dial 000," the lady said, knowing from my accent
That I would not know the emergency number.

I quickly explained, and the lady of the house then told them
  exactly where to go. She and I ran back to the scene.

The oncoming cyclist was up and about, trying to help
The other boy who had come from behind me, the boy
Who was badly hurt. By the time we got back to him I
Could already hear the sirens.
Once I knew there would be help,
I fainted next to the boy who lost his eye.

One of the paramedics woke me with smelling salts.
She asked if I needed to go to hospital.
She didn't say "the hospital" as we would.
Just "hospital," like it was a verb.

I told her that I was fine and I asked about the boy.
"He's on his way to hospital.
They will try to save his eye."
Then she asked me if I could take his bike
And call his parents to come and get it.
She gave me their number.

Suddenly, they all went away and I was alone
With a bent and broken bike, covered in the blood
Of the boy who was riding it only a few minutes before.
I walked his sad little bike home and called his parents.

Almost a month later, he came to pick up his bike.
He still had a patch on, but he was healing, and
He had been told his eye had been saved.
He thanked me for keeping his bike.

I watched him walk away, down Kensington Road
Such a trauma he had been through, all from just
Doing what kids do: they ride bikes.
I had seen the little globe of how he saw the world
Residing calmly on his face,

So far from where it should have been.

Do we ever realize how quickly our lives can change?
How brief is the time just before the bikes collide.
The distant beginnings of our strange and beautiful world
Must have felt like that, though there was no one to feel it.

In an unimaginable billion years ago
Did something collide with something else
And did everything change?
Was it so simple?
Are the small
Events of our lives
A simple reliving of that moment,
Each of them in microcosm,
Begging us to notice?
In the long silence of deep time,
When crashes combined with crashes,
What was constructed from the destruction?

# People I Must Avoid

The goal for my life was to have
No one I would ever have to avoid.
And certainly to have no one that I once knew
Who I would have to go to pains to never see again.

Now I have three. Three entire humans
Who I never want to see again.
One I can never see again,
Though we are both alive.

There is one I will see again,
But he still must be avoided
Because every sight of him is
A hatchet to my heart.
Remembering what never was
But that which we always hoped.

It is the disintegrated hope that
Must be avoided.
There will come a time when
Every person who has intersected
My life with their life will be gone,
And we will all wonder why we
Stayed away from one another.

But for now, from sixty years of living
There are three people I can never see,
Probably for the rest of my life.
What a sad inevitability.
How could it have gone differently?

# Labor Day, Cincinnati, 1978

Every Labor Day as a child,
The family would traipse away
To Cincinnati or Cleveland
For our dad's army reunion.

Every year, for one weekend,
They would all reminisce.
All of their highs and lows,
All of their loves and births
And, eventually, so many deaths.

Year by year, the reunions shrank.
Time marched across each Labor Day.
The men who had shared the worst
Loved each other forever, and they
Lived, for as long as they could , just
To see each other one more time.

The biggest thing that ever happened to
Every one of them was the one thing they
Had no need to ever talk about again.
The one unspoken subject of every reunion
Was the war.

They are bonded together forever
By Belgium, France, and Germany
By Pointe du Hoc and Arracourt
Of Crucifix Hill and Vianden.

But they met each Labor Day

For the rest of their lives,
So they could smile knowingly
Into the eyes of lives they saved.

What an honor
To be in the presence
Of so much honor,
And to witness
Such profound love.

# His Eyes

Wounded dark eyes,
Gazing into my blues.
I see myself in him.
A good part of myself.

All of the famous songs,
"A Quiet Thing"
"There Won't
 Be Trumpets"
Wonderful songs,
And so many others,
Express how when
 The moment comes
It is not fireworks
It is not noise
It is not poetry.

It is a deep intuition
Flowing like something
Carried in the blood
That just brings a slow
 Peacefulness
And fills emptinesses
That did not feel empty.

# Leaving Sydney Opera House

My favorite thing about leaving the great ship
Called Sydney Opera House, after having conducted
A performance, which I did there many hundreds of times,
Is the sensuous darkness of the night, no matter the season.

There would be few people around by the time I left.
I would stay in the Green Room by the photo of Joan
And play snooker and have a drink with my buds
For not more than an hour. I would descend to stage door.
Never "the" stage door like we say, but just stage door.

And within minutes you are out in the silent darkness
The great sails of the opera house behind you.
And birds would be in flight high above the tallest
Buildings in the CBD, as everyone calls central Sydney.
The Central Business District, never "downtown."

I would usually walk up the steps so that I could gaze back
At the most famous building of the twentieth century,
The place where we had just done a performance.
The building of so many dreams and hopes,
Where so much has been disappointing,
Where so much more lives with us forever.

# Legacies of Great Art

We do not all receive the blessing
Of exit wounds. Sometimes the pain
Stays within us for many years, if not
Forever. But we must allow the art to
Be the art, the healing force of all love.

Stop time with a kiss.
Travel in time with a story.
Release time with breath.
Feel the presence of time
By writing this very sentence.
Escape time with music.

Nothing would need
To be normalized
If the things which
Needed to be normal
Were made normal.

Art can be composed, engineered,
Planned, executed, and designed,
But it cannot, ultimately, be controlled.
I am like an art in only one way:
I am constantly into many worlds at once.

Can we forgive ourselves through art
For not being all of the many things
That we have wanted our art to be?
Because it seems like what we wanted
Each of our lives to be, but they can't.

If arts die, they will not die from neglect.
They will die from small little deaths
Created by the little cold intolerances
Of people who claim to love what you love.

We can only love what we accept.
So we must not fail to embrace the
Many truths of our art.

# Cost

The most expensive thing you will ever do
Is to trust the wrong person with your heart.
Or to listen to the person who has not yet
Listened to themselves for long enough,
Or deeply enough, to risk being really heard.
Trust anyway, but carefully.
Love anyway, but spend wisely.

# Covent Garden

Walking carefully through Covent Garden
So easy to twist your ankle on the
Old stones, trod upon for centuries.
St. James, the church for the actors and
All of the others who have tripped on these
Ancient cobbles, each of which seems to weep.

There have been tears and frustrations.
First steps and final walks, all on these rocks.
Who put them here? When were they mined?
And when were they brought
By enormous labor to be placed by hand in each of
Their places, where they would stand for hundreds
Of years, years and generations of hopes and fears?

Every word of Shakespeare hangs here, hidden
In the stones, but also Mozart and Verdi and Wagner
And Gounod, and dancers of all kinds, each taking
Enormous care over the stones, late to rehearse.

And always, there is little Eliza, a creation of another
Habitué of Covent Garden. Everywhere there is Shaw
And his Eliza, selling flowers to patrons leaving the
Great old opera house. Higgins finds her in the rain.
It all seems so real. Why does it take the creation to make
Us see the real thing with such clarity? And we walk
More carefully when we notice where we are, and why.

# A Reminder of Cruelty

Of all punishments man has devised for man.
Surely the worst is the pillory.
Imprisoning a person in their own body,
A square box all the way around their head
With just a hole for their face to stick out.
Their hands were free,
But they could not reach
Their face, could not feed themselves.
It made one totally dependent to be fed.

Sometimes they would throw sand in his face.
The pillory required a person to crawl through the streets,
Begging for food, and begging to be fed.
When people discovered that the pillory was occupied,
They would run to look at it, like people did in the South
When they heard there was going to be a lynching.

Pillory is a verb now, usually just for politics.
It is a boring word, exciting no one to action or pain.
We should remember, when we hear someone is pilloried,
That it is a word that represents centuries of pain,
A reminder of how barbaric and cruel people can be,
And could be again.

# Cy Twombly Gallery, Houston

"My five-year-old could do this"
They always seem to say.

But your five-year-old didn't do this.
And Cy Twombly did.

Maybe holding the *you*
That used to be a child
Is more important than
Holding the judgment
That is childlike simplicity.

Maybe you should get your
Five-year-old a paint brush
And a canvas and give them
The gift of your silent smile.

# Dark

It is a very dark day.
Not outside, but within me.
My soul feels like a rock
With dark icy water rushing over it.
Like those rocks up in the Tetons
The size of houses
That look like the heaviest things
On earth.

I look at this blank page
And hope that my words
As they slowly grow
From the silent white
Will heal the nameless thing
That sits at war in me.

I want to write poems of praise
To a person I aspire to love,
To talk about where they are most beautiful,
And where they make me feel young,
And how thrilling their hands feel in mine.

It feels like life is done with me today,
Or maybe that life is closing in and finding
Ways of telling me, gently but firmly,
That it won't always be as it is now.

But also that it may not always *be*.
Which means, I, the thing that is me,
Will stop at some point, probably soon,

And all pain will change to something new.
What will that mean?
It is nameless fears that we try to name
That cause every measure of every pain.

# Trusting No One

I have no idea if he did or didn't.
So please do not come here for that.
I know it was possible, but unlikely.
Or it was likely, but impossible.
Those are the two remaining options.

I know his accuser sues a lot
Which is perfectly legal, but which
Limits credibility. But if he was wronged,
He should not have been,
And he should have amends.

There was always too much joking,
Too few boundaries, too much edge.
Joking of dangerous things.
Joking of hurts.
Belittling of those perceived to have not
Enough talent to warrant seriousness.
Mean joking.

Still, if it all was a joke, even a cruel one,
Did it deserve such a severing of someone's life?
And if it was not a joke, why has it taken so long?
And why would it not be prosecuted and done with?
Something is wrong with every side of the whole thing.

I know that I miss the artistry,
Miss the ease and beauty of the voice.
I miss the most beautiful single recorded note
Of anyone of our generation.

There is a universe in that note,
And it is one that I miss.

We all had so much fun,
For so many years.
But what was lingering in the dark
Of all of those nights when we
Celebrated each other's gifts
And delighted in the next story?
Did something go terribly awry?
Or did just one ambitious attention-seeker
Find his way into the right apartment
With the right amount of booze?

# Summer Storm, Washington, D.C.

I did not want to go to Washington, D.C.
That summer, the early summer of 1978,
Because I was in a show for the first time
And I did not want to miss a moment.

But my part was small and my parents
Thought it was important to know
Our nation's capital.

You didn't book hotels in advance,
Not in those years, or not in our family.
You arrived and chose where you wanted to
Stay and found the best deal.

We found one in Tyson's Corner.
The manager was the most beautiful man
I had ever seen, so I kept inventing reasons
To take my fourteen-year-old self to the office.

I carried on an entire fantasy life with him
For the entirety of our stay in Virginia
Then I would not think about him for years
Then he would appear again as strong as ever.

The hotel was on Virginia State Road 123
Which I still remember.
1-2-3.
Every morning I would awaken last

And go with my parents to Denny's
For the same breakfast.
"You always know what you are getting,"
Mom would say.

Then we would drive into Washington
Across Highway 50 and see a different set
Of sights each day.
And each day we would drive across the bridge
By Roosevelt Island and the Kennedy Center,
Then still considered "new," was on our left.
I never got tired of looking at it.
I wanted to know the name of everything.
Hall of States. Hall of Nations. Grand Foyer.
Tidal Basin.

*In this temple, as in the hearts of the people for whom he saved the Union, the memory of Abraham Lincoln is enshrined forever.*

Gathering
The nation's memories
Within our own.
I wanted to see
One more place
Before we drove
Back to Indiana.
It was the late afternoon before we
Would leave the next morning before dawn,
The last day I would
Ever see the gorgeous manager.
I wonder if he is still alive.

Library of Congress and Folger Shakespeare.
Those were the destinations that my fourteen years

Most wanted, more than any other museums.
My parents did not consider Shakespeare or Congress
To be places for them.

This was long before I realized how intimidated
They were by education, and how much it would
Separate them from their children,
So anything related to libraries frightened them.
All of the feelings come back when I remember
That night when I made us go to the Library.

Sign of the times: we parked on the grounds
Of the Capitol Building
The Capital of the United States of America.
Today you cannot get anywhere near it
In a car. But there we were on the grounds.

"I'll wait here," Dad said.
Preferring to sit in the car
Than seeing the Library of Congress.
I protested that I wanted him to see it.

We were in the Library, taking a tour,
Which to my surprise and theirs,
My parents loved.
Suddenly the electricity went out.
We huddled towards a window.

A storm had blown in.
Violent, the color of smoke.
Green and black.
"The Washington Monument has been evacuated,"
Someone yelled. Tornados dropped all around.

We were safe in the Library.
But the storm was terrifying.
Wind and crashing rain.
My dad kept saying, "Look at that"
As though one could look at anything else.

The storm subsided.
And we made our way back to the car.
On the grounds of the Capitol.
Some policemen were talking.
Mom screamed.

A tree had fallen on our car.
Smashed it flat.
All four tires relieved of their air.
I wonder how it must have sounded.
The tree cracking under the wind,
Breaking every window.

It was, of course, my fault.
I had insisted we be in the place
At that moment.
But my parents never once
Blamed me.

# Santa Barbara

California has hills stacked liked books
Pointing towards the sea.
When you drive PCH towards Malibu
You can see them, but not only there.
Stretching towards the see is what they do.
Green or gold, depending on the season.
Unearthly beauty. Did the sea rise to greet them?
Everything exceptional about us is in California.
Or it used to be. The western promise is fading.

Mother and daughter, thirty years apart, begging to die.
I knew her mom because I called her Grandma,
Though she wasn't my grandparent.
I never knew mine. Born too late.
But when they asked me at school about grandparents,
I told the teacher that Mary was my grandma.
And the teacher laughed. But I asked Mary
If I could call her Grandma,
And she said she would love it.
I never called her anything else.

Now Mary's daughter is older than
Mary was ever allowed to be.
I never thought they were alike, mother and daughter,
But now they are.
Like her mother, the daughter is now a
Tired fleshly machine, gaunt and frail.
Age has erased her vitality.
She was named after the pain of another Mary,
Dolores, but we called her Dee.

For me, she was California.
Vital, healthy, always growing and vibrant.
Now, though, she waits in the pretty place
For the great slipping away,
The dousing of the candle that was her life.

Are we what we *do*
Or are we really who we are?
Dee was everything I thought life should be.
What will I do without her?

# Emily Knwarreye

Dots and strokes.
Thrilling energy
Wind passing over the canvas.
My first morning in Sydney.
Jet-lagged beyond belief.
I walked to the gallery in the park.
The one that spells Michelangelo
As Michael Angelo
Like he was from Long Island.

I walked in and around the first corner
To the left, starting into the darkness.
And there is was, my first sign of Emily.
It couldn't fit into one line of sight.

You had to view it slowly
Like any landscape,
Because not only was it large.
It was simply too beautiful
To be seen all at once.

# Epiphany in Central Park

I had an epiphany in Central Park.
Epiphanies are when you think a thought,
And after that thought
None of your other thoughts are the same.
Real epiphanies are rare.

Central Park is the one place in
The confabulation that is New York
Where you can still feel old ghosts.
They hover there, far from wherever they were.
Far from their apartments.

Long after the opening nights
The ones that hurt or the ones
That bought the country houses,
So that they could feel like they are
In Central Park when they leave New York.

Everyone escapes to the park
But it is the one uncrowded place.
And the spirits linger there.
Rodgers, Hammerstein, Herbert
(There's his statue right there)
Edna Ferber
(Why do I always think of her in Central Park?)

I think of all of the photos of Kate.
Of Katharine sitting in the castle of the park,
Reading the paper, probably reading about herself.
Wasn't her name probably in the paper every week?

The park still holds Greta Garbo,
Comden and Green,
Bacall, Michael Bennett,
James Levine, before the fall,
When he lived at the San Remo.

Tennessee Williams in the Ramble.
*Angels in America* hanging in the ether
Before it was written it was probably
Just an idea in the park, another epiphany.
Bethesda Fountain, Prior Walter's favorite place.

I've had such dreams in the park,
Dreams of many years.
The morning after seeing
*Into the Woods* for the first time.
That original cast.
One November night.
No one is alone.
The morning after I went to the park.
Dreams. Dreams.

Arriving back to New York after England.
Months of chasing a boy who was not for me.
I had conducted *Rigoletto* on my last night
In gorgeous Oxford, another dreaming place.
My heart was in New York, but it was impossible
To ignore Oxford, the endless grasses and misty
Forests kissing the ancient stones.

But I flew back to New York
For my first jet-lagged June morning.
Off to Central Park for a walk.

A perfect morning.
You could feel all of England
New and old,
In the green canopy.

Near the castle, but not in the Ramble,
I hear a woman calling for her dog.
"Rex! Rex!" and all I could think was
"King! King!" but I started looking for
Rex because the woman seemed eager to find him.

She was a disembodied voice coming
From several directions until suddenly
We were face to face.
She was in her eighties at least.
Very athletic. Warm and beautiful face.
Someone you instantly love.

Then I saw her wrist.
The faded tattooed numbers.
She had survived a camp.
She didn't talk about it.

"Isn't it the most gorgeous morning!"
She said, bursting with joy.
I asked about Rex.

"Oh, I don't have a dog.
I just pretend I'm calling my dog.
In case someone I come across
Is not very nice.
But you are lovely,
So I don't have a dog!"

I will never forget her.

On my epiphany day
Much more recently,
Along the Mall,
Near Bethesda Fountain,
A Chinese man was playing the erhu
Like I had seen in Shanghai decades ago.

He was so small, so hungry, and had
Traveled so far. What was his life?
Did he travel in from Teaneck or Flushing,
Maybe Great Neck?

He played erhu in Central Park
To make enough money to feed his family.
I had made my life making music.
Privileged beyond measure.

So I handed him the $100 I had in my pocket.
He cried. His day had been made.
The old woman would be gone now,
And this Chinese man will not live
More than ten more years.

Did I make one of his days easier?
I hope I did.
My old lady chasing Rex
Changed my whole life.
So I paid her back.

# Fireflies

When the fireflies came in the '70s summer,
I went to my favorite childhood hill.
It wasn't really a hill, but if you were small,
It felt as big as a real hill will.

From up there I could see
The older trees in town,
The ones that heard people
Talk about the Civil War.

At night, when no one could see me,
Sometimes I would take off all of my clothes
And sit on the hill looking at the stars.

Wasn't I eaten alive by chiggers?
I don't remember.
My little white naked body in the grass,
Would wonder what was out there in the night.

The sky is so quiet that it demands
We surrender to its silence.
Once, totally naked, I fell asleep
With the grass tickling my neck.
At first it felt like an airport.
Then I was in an old house.
Then I was in a tree, way up in it,
Watering dead flowers.

Another time, when I kept my clothes on,
The fireflies looked like cameras flashing

In a huge theater,
The ones with stacked balconies.
It looked like they were taking my picture,
Telling me that my life
Might somehow involve a stage.

I could see them, out there in wolf's mouth
Back in those years before judgment,
Before doubt,
Before wounds,
Before fear,
Before the almosts.
Before joy, too.

If your noble act is unseen,
It is still noble.
Replaying failures,
Fueling doubts,
Walking into empty rooms,
Must all cease someday.

When trees begin to die,
You tend the soil, not the tree.
There is no escaping time's prison.
The trees I climbed in my childhood
Are no longer welcoming me,
But the ones that are still standing,
Must still have the descendants of
The same caterpillars I loved at five?

The highest question is this:
What do we notice?

The shape of clouds
Even at night, above the fireflies.
Why do we not taste
This miracle every day?

Even in our old little town
There were burned bridges
And unlit frightened alleyways.
Old churches and cemeteries
Like the one in the last scene of *Our Town*.
He knew of what he wrote.

The day we buried our mother.
Christmastime 2001.
Months after the heart-cracking fury.
Winter rain.
Cold but pleasant,
More mist than rain.
But we needed umbrellas,
As my dearest friends said,
"*Our Town*" and we all smiled.

A cascade of random circumstances.
Why do differences matter so much?
Differences do not judge; they invite.
Differences are happy urgencies.
The apologies needed but never received
Must not be given access.

Back on the nights of the fireflies,
I had my childhood dreams
And those moments came.
The dark theaters with their

Mysterious flickering lights and
Joys and sorrows and hopes and almosts.

Beauty stops your breath
Because it stops everything.
There is nothing, ultimately,
*Except* beauty.
The incredible beauty to which
We constantly aspire to inspire.

Let me enter your peace
As I wanted to enter mine.
Your soul was soft where I was not.
And I fear I hardened you where you most tender.
I was your chapter, but you were my book.
But the fireflies return, and still I look.

# Flaws

I was a reading a book,
Loving its world,
Reveling in its images,
Lost in its parallel world.

When suddenly there it was:
A typo that jumped off the
Page like a fart at a funeral.
Did no one edit this book?

The steering wheel of my new
Car, the only part of it I
Can feel, has a small rip on
Its underside.

A whole world of the wheel
Is doing exactly what it ought.
But my obsession is with the
Flaw, the tiny thing that does not belong.

We get angry at the flaws,
The parts we did not ask for.
What the flaws need is love,
And maybe a little help.

I stopped reading the book
That I was loving
Just because it had a typo.

Why could I not just

Keep reading and realize
That one little flaw did not
Diminish the whole book?

Who throws something out
Just because it has a blemish?

# Fort Worth, March 2023

What was it worth, really?
Did it ever mean anything except cows?
Will Rogers.
Fort Worth is the true nowhere of Texas,
If only because it so much wants to be the center or
Always, seemingly, anywhere but where it is.

Yes, this March, on a little street in the west,
It feels like the most beautiful place ever.
The sun was setting.
I walked for many blocks,
Up and down hills.
By a church, gracious houses,
Slightly too close together,
And several mansions, but
None of them so huge,
Like Dallas or Houston
Or the awful McMansions of Austin.

Finishing my big circle,
Where I saw acorns longing to be oaks,
Where I saw the leaning gold light kiss the west
Where I saw not one other soul walking.
I found total silence, and not even a leaf blower,
For once.

As I circled back to where I started,
A little commotion drew my eye towards a treetop.
Four cardinals were talking to each other and,
With great clarity, made their quiverings known to me.

They must have been cold, unable to stop moving.

They were trying to tell me something.
I know many people think cardinals carry souls
The souls who have passed on.
That cardinals have their own little energies,
But they also absorb those who are trying to reach us.
Through the cardinals, our loved ones can find us.

Who was it?
Which four souls were trying to find me?
And why?
I stopped for many minutes and watched them.
It was more than watching.
It was a stillness.
The type of beauty
That finds us so rarely.

The birds were happy to see me.
They were loving and mysterious.
They made me stop and watch them.
But they made me do much more.
They made me pause and notice where I was,
That I was under a sky,
That there were trees of huge beauty,
That the light leading us west is a god.

And they made me smile at their happiness,
Which quickly became mine.
I was, I told myself,
In that moment with my cardinal quartet,
Supremely, eternally, happy,
As I seemed in the moment

To have always been and, for a moment,
I would always be.

Worth.

# Dear One
## Frances Marzio (1947–2022)
## Read at her memorial at
## Museum of Fine Arts, Houston

We repeat, just as music does.
This was your repetition, dear one:
Happiness.
Stop.
Retreat.
Happiness.
Stop.

Those raised with absence
Forever seek their missing beauty.
And often the beautiful
Must be solitary, quiet, and unadorned.
Gray, white, and black.
Let life be the color.

There were many days
When you had to hold up the sky.
Now you know,
How you were loved
And how we cared.
Then and now.

You were inwardness.
Perceiving all, disclosing none.
You knew the power of silence,
And the seduction of amazement.

And you, dear one,
Knew a great, selfless, generous love.
Who filled your life with everything you
Learned from art about love.

There was only one place where you could be met:
In a small willing space,
Where you would open a door
To a small shimmering light.
Where you could hold a hand
So lightly I would weep.

You loved those dark roads,
Where ancient fires burn.
Moored to the highest tide.
Art held all your love, because
Art begs for nothing except
For one soul
To look at it.

A poem is the last gift I can give
For the friendly hours we carried.
That single morning at the Frick
When you were so happy.
Our dozen afternoons at the old Whitney
Or at the Morgan.
And the unforgettable
Numberless days near this spot.

In ten thousand years
Someone might be able
To see all of us
Still in movement,
Like those who now look at old stars

Through great machines.
We look now at dying stars
Which means they are looking at us.

The light that casts shadows
In old caves,
The light that makes us paint,
And take photos,
And sculpt,
And write operas,
And cry over books,
Is a light we all share.
Art passes through nature,
Not nature through art.

Farewell, dear one.
The heroes of Alexandria, Rome, and Athens
Are watching you
Because you watched them.

# We are Not as Funny as We Used to Be

I heard each of these sentences before I was five:

People in hell want ice water.
As nervous as a cat in a room full of rockers.
Their cornbread ain't done in the middle.
That makes my ass want to dip snuff.

As helpful as a handful of hemorrhoids in a hurricane.
Finer than frog hair split four ways.
Colder than a well-digger's ass in Idaho.
Not all of his oars were in the water.

Running around like a lost fart in a perfume factory.
Useless as a screen door on a submarine.
If assholes could fly this would be an airport.
Butter my butt and call me a biscuit.
She's the town bicycle.
That dog don't hunt.
If every problem looks like a nail,
Then you will always have a hammer.
As full as a tick on a slow-moving dog.
He's walking like he's got an egg broke up him.

# Geist

That word of words.
Everything we do in life
Involves some meaning
Of that simple word.

But what a shadow it casts.
The word spirit, *geist* in German,
Means too many things besides spirit:
Ghost, mind, soul.
But they are all vital
To every moment.

Using it in professional life,
Where it describes art at every level,
Where *soul* is the only honest word,
But we use spirit so that we lose
Any religious context. But *spirit* then
Is described as pompous by those looking
For definitions of quite another kind.

We do not live our lives with ghosts.
Obviously we use our minds,
But minds are not inspiring.
It is the spirit that inspires,
And the soul that warms itself.

I will use the words that work,
As should we all, whether or not
They are the words of the moment.

# Adolf Hitler

I am standing, right now,
As this pen scratches over my diary,
Over the place where Hitler died.
The bunker, except it is gone.
There is no marker, no site of martyrdom.
He died as he lived, in a hole full of hatred.

He does not deserve a poem.
The destruction he caused is neither
Forgivable nor over.

But he is someone we can never ignore
Or forget, as much as we wish we could.
As time passes, we forget why he happened.
His name is used now without responsibility,
And without real knowledge about who he was.

Do we know just how hateful he was?
Sure. That is the easy part of understanding him.
Hatred is all too easy.

What we forget about him is that he had a mind,
Not just a hateful heart. He saw enemies everywhere.
The Treaty of Versailles lived in his heart with venom.
He didn't care if Germany was humiliated.
He cared only that *he* was humiliated.
He wanted to make Germany great again,
Not because it was great, but because he could be needed.

He could blame Jews for everything because

Jews have been blamed for everything for centuries.
He stepped into a blazing fire with just the right fuel,
At just the right moment, screaming about Aryans
And Master Races and Romaní, and bloodlines, and
Those born with no limbs, or homosexuals, or anyone
On whom he could feel powerful hope for his hatred.

But he knew *exactly* how to do it. He never had to
Explicitly say what he hated because everyone could
Hear his dog whistles. They knew his symbols because
They taught all of them to him. He was a good student.

What if he had died or been killed in 1939?
Would his underlings still have carried out his orders?
Would there still have been a Holocaust?
Or better yet, what if he had died in 1933,
Before he set the groundwork of laws
That made the Holocaust all too easy?
He was smart. He knew exactly what he was doing.

Tens of millions dead because of him.
European life drawn to a halt.
The entire world drawn into war.
Other countries taking Hitler's lead
And decent people saw their lives changed
And could even see them disappearing.

He was not the only horror of the twentieth century.
But he was the only one whose death site I am
Right at this moment standing over, on a beautiful
Clear day in Berlin. There is a small sign and a few
Tourists, but where his life ended is now a parking lot.
And, most beautifully, it is a playground.

Patrick Summers

A few children are giggling on swings
While their parents have a picnic nearby.
Do they know where they are?
I hope they do and I hope they don't.

# Jackie

Something in the feeling of Avenue Foch
Always at a particular time of day.

Strange that Paris was where I felt the safest.
When I felt there was no safety anywhere.

The angle of the buildings brought it to me.
I always said I could not remember it.

Jumping out of the back of the limousine,
Which looked to many like attempted escape.

But a piece of my husband's skull disappeared.
And all I did was try to save it to save him.

But there was nothing about that day that I
Will ever forget. I remember each face.

The heart of the world was broken that Friday.
And they wonder, I know they wonder.

If I ever went back to Dallas.
What they will never know

Is that I did. Ten years later.
1973, not on the real day.

But it was November.
We flew to Love Field

And we drove the route
All over again. I made them wait

On the spot where it happened.
The place where the air cracked.

And the world split open, just like
The feeling on the Avenue Foch.

# Katy Trail, Dallas

You'd think Katy had something to do with the city in Texas.
But the trail name is from the Kansas-Texas rail line. K. T.
Everything in Texas means something else.

Forever stained by a dead President.
The great national trauma
That never heals.
Will Dallas ever mean more than that?

The most beautiful March day.
Perfect air and infinite sky.
Part of the firmament,
Walking the whole Katy Trail.
Reverchon to Mockingbird.
Names you only find in Dallas,
A place that isn't considered beautiful.
But it is beautiful. Hidden beauty is still beauty.

Studying *Parsifal*.
*The Fisher King*.
Things that mean other things.
Deep expansive study of all of the symbols
That plague our lives. The wounds unhealed.
The longings unfulfilled.
Listening as I walk.
And passing me constantly.
Are the most gorgeous men
In the world, shirts left at home.

The ancient myths.

The hero of the twentieth century,
So Jung said, was Parsifal.
The innocent fool.

Yet my foolishness is not innocent at all.
I fool my eyes into seeking the parts they desire.
Staring down the most beautiful men.
Their pecs, their marbled arms,
Their confidence in appearing almost naked.
Imagining them in ecstasy, would that have been
Before or after they put on those tight shorts
And decided to go to the trail for a walk?

The beautiful doggies are everywhere.
And the men who have dogs get the best ogle.
Because we can pretend we are looking at their dog.
While the eye never needs to go above the waist.

I once saw a little girl get lost on the trail.
A little redhead who couldn't fully walk
But she could run.
She had gotten away from her mother
And wondered onto the Katy Trail.

I tried to help her, to approach her.
She was afraid of me, afraid of masculinity.
Other men tried to help.
She would only allow a woman to be near her.

A lady stopped jogging and picked her up.
We asked her name. She would only cry.
She was probably too young to even know her name.
Turns out her name was Katy. Bizarre.

Her mother had fallen asleep and the little girl
Went out their patio door and got lost.
The police found the mother, frantic,
Looking everywhere for her little girl.
The police told her to lock her door.
That this could have gone very badly
If there "hadn't been nice people" on the trail.
The mother said there are only nice people there.

# Knowing

I know Sydney, New York, San Francisco
Los Angeles, Honolulu, Aldeburgh
Paris, Berlin, Rome
Bloomington, Chicago, St. Louis,
Evansville, Indiana, of all places, I know it well.
Meaning, I notice when parts of it are missing
When I return.

I know Cincinnati, and I strangely often miss it.
I know Aspen and Denver and a bit of Boulder.
I know Santa Fe and Fredericksburg, Texas
To the point of knowing people who own shops.
There's a strange place for me to know:
New Harmony, Indiana
One of the sweetest places in the world.
And one never tires of it.
A piece of me stays there always.

Two places I know really well are
Washington, D.C., and Baton Rouge.
Isn't that weird?

Tangier, thanks to a friend.
Lisbon, Tel Aviv, Jerusalem
Barcelona, Seville, Madrid
Vienna, Bregenz
Shanghai in a certain era.
Hong Kong
Melbourne
Moscow, the area around my hotel,

    And Café Pushkin.
Leura and Katoomba,
    The fireplace in Lilianfels, where
    I spend every night of my dreams,
    Where it is coldest in July.
Copenhagen and Cardiff
    Places where I was sad.
Mexico City
    Where I was once so anxious I
    Could not sleep for three days
    Through no fault of Mexico.
One night in Nanjing,
    Where all of history seemed to sit.
    So many ghosts in so much pain
    Were watching us in Nanjing.

Such privilege, to know these places.
To know where to eat and where to sit
And have coffee and tea and write.
Where to go for the best view, like
Mirablau in Barcelona.
Is there a more beautiful spot anywhere?

But what does knowing mean?
I only know my home, and my home
Is in none of those places.
Knowing means certainty.
I am unsure of everything.

I know all of these places,
But I do not know the one thing
I most long to know.

# Krakatoa

The sound heard around the world.
The primal urges of our only home
Are hard at work in the straits of Sunda.

The word people love to say.
Deep earthly fires rumble still.
Anyer lighthouse shining always.

Orange embers reach for the sky
And fall onto the black nothingness.
The son of Krakatoa is growing.

Twenty feet every year.
It knows nothing of our time.
It hurled itself into the sky.

Changing the skies of the world
For many years.

# Ruining the World

Leaf-blowers fucking with every morning
Trash and shit chucking their airborne warning.

Machinery vomiting horrible scents.
Noise that is worth, I guess, more than my silence?

When Voltaire told us to make gardens grow,
He did *not* think flaming fast air apropos.

Depressing to think that they never will go,
More pleasant to sink on a scorching hot dildo.

Disheartening to know that we'll never be free of them.
And worse to pretend that we ever have needed them.

And what of the creatures in the underbrush,
Feeding themselves on what ought to be lush?

Or bunnies just trying to love the grass,
Running from dust being blown up their ass?

We've made normal what should be a crime,
To steal the silence of a day in its prime.

If you blow it from *here* to over there,
Who takes it from over *there*, and to where?

Tomorrow someone will blow it back,
Like a sexless nymphomaniac.

We thought we knew about Dante's hell,
Until we hear from wherever we dwell:

The sound of Satan farting his dinner,
Hour after hour 'til joy is thinner.

Blowing the leaves must scratch some itch,
But whoever invented it sure was a bitch.

I hear them and instantly I'm in a rage,
I'd blow up each on the world's biggest stage.

These sounds will go on for the rest of our lives,
Cutting through peace like rusty old knives.

No day without these horrid machine screams,
Like dragons and snakes in horrible dreams.

For ever so long our ears will ache.
What is so wrong with a fucking rake?

# Lost Brothers

I just met him.
Only two times now, on Sundays.
With our dear elderly friend whom we both love,
Who reminds us that life and love are a river that flows.

We both lost men
Who were too young to die
When we were too young to lose them.
Our own deaths commenced on those long crying days.

Deep in lost time,
Ten thousand explosions ago,
Generations before our parents united
Our brothers were part of our lives and each other's.

The Pacific took both.
My brother died within sight of Mussel Rock,
Where the great earth once shook for about a minute.
He knew the danger of the shore, but not the danger within him.

Anchorage, Cook Inlet Mud Flats
Took his brother, who was trying to see the view.
Of Turnagain Arm, hiking with a friend, who got out.
He ignored the dangers he would never have allowed others.

Kincaid Park, Fire Island.
Not that Fire Island, but the one in Alaska.
He misread the tide that he knew better than anyone.
One slip in the mud, one rock too many, and the sea is merciless.

We untie the strings
And release the long ropes that bind us.
Do they look to us now from wherever they are,
And wish we were happier, wish we were together, even?

The great ocean, unfeeling.
Collected tears from all who knew them.
The salt that sits on the tongues of whales used to be ours.
The scent of the seawater, the kelp, and
   the seals still bring him home.

Joseph Hugh, Phillip Anthony
Both with younger brothers who followed,
Men to whom they were heroes, and who loved nature.
We walked a thousand miles together, all over the world.
   Not enough.

He is beautiful.
This tiny wounded enigma.
He has been hardened and hurt by life.
But he still holds a belief that a great love will appear.

As we live on,
We realize they never leave.
They stay with us in ceaseless brotherhood.
Locked together forever in the churning fires of the earth.

# Mansefeldt, August 2022
## For Dian and Harlan Stai

Their voices are in the wind: Old German women praying.

    They stand sentinel with God in the old stones.

    They pray old German prayers and German hymns

> *Lobe den Herren*
> *Der alles so herrlich regieret*
> (Praise to the Lord, who rules over everything)

Their old words seep into the whispering loam.

The women knew war, so they could fight with nature,

    And know where within the earth the harmony lies.

You can hear them in the grand silence of the guarding trees,

    See the long hot skirts they sewed.

    Watch them convincing men what to value.

    Did they know they were building for centuries?

        That their stones silently watched men leave for the Great War?

Did the stones know the Great War was not the last?

Their childhood classrooms were at the feet of their elders.

When the final oil lamp went out in Palmyra or Sumer,

    The night sky was no different

    From what we see now from the Manse.

    What scale is dignity?

    One imagines Jerusalem before the Temple.

Though we want it to be water, imagination is fire,

    Earth's fires singed every red rock,

    Born of fundamental shifts and ancient powers.

    It is hot there now, as it was then, as it will probably always be.

I follow the path of the holy fool,

    Moving from time to space to firmament,

    Longing for achievement that never comes.

I seek the empty fullness of nature,

    My mind whirring like a puppy.

    Mansefeldt effortlessly slows all.

Great creative fires are made, not begotten.

And they carry the burden of conscience.

From the Manse the entire cosmos can be seen.

Reminding us that we can't know

And what we don't.

Mary and her son saw the same stars.

Moonlight is sunlight somewhere; we are all mere reflections.

Costumed dolls, Bibles read for centuries,

Photos of the unknown, who all
loved and lost and cried and prayed.

Volumes of Shakespeare bring moral agency to
an orphaned world.

There is Calvinist beauty.

Mahler's endlessly repeating search.

The sheep dance by their barn, happy and fat.

Metal soldered into stone, the old way.

Sunset at Mansefeldt enlarges something delicately remarkable,

An image of our highest capacities.

Everywhere there are disciplined kindnesses.

We participate in eternity.

Gentle simpler souls rest under a chapel of trees,

Our innocent accompanying friends:

We are their whole life. So much pure love.

Change is not always an advance.

This ancient place is stimulus to inspiration.

It has no artificial language.

Arms open wide to all except the lazy.

It is simplifying but not simple.

It holds divine intent.

The moral mirror beckons us, and

The community of excellence, beauty, and holiness hovers.

# Mark Wagner

Everyone remembers their first redhead.
Because no one knew, but everyone knew,
The great Lucy on television.
Mark never made it past his teenage years
So he is forever young to all who knew him,
But few people knew him.

Except for his mom and sister
Mark was our town's only redhead.
Quiet. Sweet. Painfully shy and withdrawn.
He was always looking for a voice.
And loved singing, both his own and others.
He held up our gentle world of
Small houses in small towns.
The only people with big houses owned
Funeral homes or furniture stores, but

Mark had a shy tenor voice at first
When he sang his little body got bigger.
He had no muscle on him but no fat either.
He was a lean little boy who always seemed
Wary of the world, like he was expecting you
To hurt him, or awaiting the next time you might.

I was shocked when he went to the Navy
Instead of music school. I thought he wanted
To be a singer.
But like thousands before him,
He wanted to prove that he was a man.

So he went to Pearl Harbor.
He wrote me a couple of times
And there was nothing to read between the lines.
He would not say anything real in his letters.
There was no hint of the pain he must have been in.

The call came. The horrible call.
Everything was mystery.
Mark was dead. He had been shot
On a ship in Pearl Harbor.
No one could understand.
We were not at war.
Had someone killed Mark?
Why? Did someone figure out he was gay
Before he did?

A few days later we gathered at the funeral home.
But his body had not arrived. It was late.
We waited and waited. So much anger.
His body had been flown with honor guard
From Hawaii and they were late.

Finally a hearse arrived.
We all watched Mark's family
As they watched him arrive.
They had none of the normal
Time alone with their dead son and brother.

No one talked about it, not ever.
But how did Mark die?
Could that sweet boy not accept
The beauty of his own self?
A trigger was pulled, his pain ended,
And ours began.

# Mauthausen

Just outside of Linz, Upper Austria
On a gentle and verdant hillside,
Lies Mauthausen, one of those places
That humanity can never, should never,
Will never, forget.
How could we? It must remain unforgettable.

I kept seeing the name, somehow,
In little graffitos around Berlin,
In shop names around Vienna.
The name seemed to pop up.

This chilled me: I was
Taking a long walk in Vienna,
Behind the Karlskirche
Towards Elizabethviertel
When I glanced over to an entrance,
One like thousands of others in Vienna.

It was a survivor's trust, a nonprofit
Devoted to preventing another Mauthausen.
Why does this name haunt me so completely?
There were many places of horror during those years.

But somehow, Mauthausen remains in front of me.
Never behind me, as though I had been there.

I decided, on one recent day, that I must go there.
I drove myself to Mauthausen,
As I could not bear to take a comfortable train

To such a terrible deathly lonely tragic place.

It has a strange beauty, because it is a sweet spot.
Which must have been true then, when it was all horror.
I climbed the terrible steps and tried
With no success at all
To imagine the daily terror
That climbed there.

Are their souls all still there
Watching over those of us
Who want to remember them
While wishing we could forget?

Did no one nearby hear their screams?
In the beautiful breeze of the late afternoon,
I believe I can hear them in the silence.
The long terrible crying screaming silence.

# Millennial

Privileged millennial in a job he hates.
Fighting against all authority for no reason
Other than trying to find his own nobility.

He articulates anger at this or that, on to the
Next thing before you've heard the first.
He rages and machinates and fulminates,
But when he really needs his outrage,
It will all have been spent.

He could make his life so much better than it is.
While he rages against the wrong machine,
He sees enemies where none have been.
Studying, practicing, making friends, so sure
That his life would go a certain way it didn't.

The machine has no interest in him.
It eats everything that gets near it and
Those who find happiness around it find it
Because they know the truth of the machine.
They don't try to get it to be something it is not.

We place the yoke on ourselves.
So we cannot turn around and yell,
"Look, I am tethered!" or "How dare you
Place this yoke upon me and turn away?"

The machine is a horror, so stop pretending
It is gorgeous and it owes you everything.
You are supposed to rage against the dying light,

Remember?
So why spend it raging on shit?

# Montmartre Déjà

We were walking on Rue Lepic
My first trip to Paris.
We had been walking all day.
From Châtelet to Montmartre.
Hours and hours.

The Parisian light was goldening.
We found a perfect spot.
Paris spread out below us.
The sun dipped behind the chimneys
And many famous silhouettes.

The moment was captured.
Three friends, all of us young
In love, not with each other,
But with all that life held in front of us,
And with the long carefree weekend in Paris.

We were walking down Montmartre
To find a taxi to take us to St. Germain
Where we would have a late dinner outside.
But as we turned to descend a staircase,
I was struck with a déjà vu, the strongest of my life.

In an instant, with no time to analyze it.
I was in woman in the 1920s, who was
Truly suffering. A cruel lover at home was
Giving her a need to hurt herself.

She did, too, very badly. She threw

Her own body down the huge stairs of Montmartre.
She was hoping just to cause enough harm
To get her husband to notice her.

But she did not count on hitting her head
With the force of falling. She was dead by
The time she got to the first landing,
Where she was found the next morning.
By a man walking up to Montmartre.

Just like we had walked over Paris that day.
This man was planning to go up to see the view.
He found the terrible sight. The broken neck.
The blood that was already dried from no force
Left to pump it. Paris has seen everything.

# Murmurations

The best word for one of the world's best things.
Our last beautiful living remnant of a Mesozoic world.
The birds evolved this way of keeping themselves safe.
Their ballets in the sky deserve all of our awe,
Especially in a world where so little awe is warranted.

They hypnotize each other, swirling around the sky
A welcome gift to the heavens from our in-between space.
Mesmerizing protections of each other.
What fish do but we can almost never see,
The birds do in the sky
Improvising their collective wonder.
Each bird connects to seven around them
But we cannot fully know why.

In murmuration, if you can get close to them,
They sound like ocean waves.
The divinity of nature danced in front of us.
Each starling accepting the idea formation
For only one reason we can imagine: to save one.
To keep one bird safe, they create art.
At least it is art for us, because we cannot conceive
Of what they are doing in any other way.

Their feeding, or their protection, is beauty to us.
Maybe they are just playing. What about that?
Maybe it is simply fun up there, following the
Caprice of the breeze, feeling the sun dipping down
Sending the air itself alight with new smells and humors.

They are like the alleyways of a body
A whole circulatory system of their own.
Or a solar system, or the roots of a tree
Following itself through the universe,
Looking for itself, or finding itself?
We can never know,
Which keeps it unutterably beautiful.
How gorgeous to never know.

We would be better if we said the word
*Murmuration* once a day.

# Near Dover Hill

Summer of 1975, a halcyon day
Though we didn't know it then
Except, I think we did.

We were both twelve.
In those years before sex
Before even thinking about it.
Me with Brian. Inseparable.

There was an old house near the
End of Reinhart Road, where you turn right
On Wildman, though no one around ever called it
Wildman.

It was just "the old road to Dover Hill."
Anyway, there where the road goes
Into deep forest on its long way
Over to Dover Hill and cemeteries
And trash landfills and scary things.

We were on bicycles, of course.
We went everywhere on bicycles
Which is why just a few years later,
When the bicycles flew across the moon
In that gorgeous film, it spelled *forever* to us.

We left our bikes on the gravel road
On that hot Saturday in the summer.
The house was halfway up the hill
Old white clapboard, like ten thousand others.

One lit candle in the window would have been
Seen all over the valley, back in the day,
Back when there was life in the house.

No one had lived in it for years.
They hadn't sold it; they just left.
Or there was no one to inherit it.
A long-dead radio from the 1940s
Was still on the porch,
Worth money without its weathering.

An immediate dream arose.
I would build a house on that hill,
Or maybe on some other hill,
And look at the distant light
And wonder how everyone was.

I had only twelve summers
Of dreaming back then
So my dreams were not yet big.
I could picture the sunsets
And the long morning coffees.
On mornings like this one I would
Just breathe the breeze and plan my day.

With my eyes of only a dozen years,
I saw myself as an old man,
Proudly looking over this very valley
And remembering the long life of
Happiness in the house. Funny.
Not this house, I immediately dreamed
But a new house on this spot.
It seemed to me the finest spot for a house
That there could ever be.

Brian and I walked up the hill,
Which seemed to our little legs to be
A small mountain.
The house was always far away,
A destination seen for miles.
We must have planned our bike ride
For many weeks, to go up,
Up to the house on the hill.

Red and silver maples and sycamores
Were happily untrimmed, enjoying their liberty.
The spirit of the world was once in this house.
There was great happiness here.
There were still bed frames,
Where babies were conceived.
They held each other sweetly on some
Distant morning before the world
Plunged towards two wars, no more.
Terrible news from wartime fronts
Once reached this house.
You could still hear the crying.
On our morning, curtains were still
Blowing with the breeze.
It was the quietest place on earth.

Nighttime in this house was not simply
An absence of day.
It was a time for expansion,
For cooling,
For total silence to reclaim
The roar of tractors in the valley.
Nature was swiftly reclaiming it.
The house was leaning on its foundations,
Its bones creaking and stooped

Like someone who has lived longer
Than they wanted to live.

Someday, only a few seasons more,
It would fall down completely and little boys
On their bikes would ride by and see nothing
But another hill.

But that day, that lone morning of my
Childhood, it was the greatest place
To ever be, and no dream could ever
Have been bigger than to stay in that house
And capture all of the time it had seen in its
Long life.

# October Questions

October words are in color.
The wind, after talking to the air,
Invites leaves down.

October once gave me wings.
The moldy leaves in California, in a
Long-ago October, were everything.
Was it a blessing or a lesson?

I broke my own heart.
Penitence is a breeze across our forehead,
A thing to notice but not feel.
Have I absolved myself?

Suddenly, one morning, the heat is gone
And the moisture in the air bends.
October has lighter air than September.
Where does the heat go?

The earth is shifting
On an invisible axis.
Who figured that out?
Quiet dignity, not like spring,
Sits in the infinite art of the sky.

Will the summer light remember me?
The new mornings are mute and easy,
With shorter shadows and lighter days.
October releases the ghosts of the year.

The shallow part of the lake
Sways with short reeds,
Little bones in a slight grave,
Or crushed petals from flowers
That never knew their end was nigh.

Mystic sexual essences
Live in autumn's colors.
Ancient waters in which one swims,
Threaten each season, save autumn,
When faded springs pour forth.

Walking in the quiet dark night in California.
Through expectant silences that smell nude.
There is new sea air and old fog,
Slippery lichen that smells green.
How do we learn how green smells?

Red and orange leaves finally at their rest.
Washed, eventually, to the strait,
Then the bay,
Then on to the sea.
Or do they just melt back into the earth?
What happens to them?
What follows this newest October?

# Old Women

How rarely we talk to
The many who live within us.
They wait patiently in their old houses
On hills and by ponds their husbands built.
They stay where they loved the most.

One of the dozen old
German women who live in me
Went to the window this morning
And cried.

But the Irish men and Dutch women
Who also live in me,
They do a lot of laughing
And drinking
And crying
And wondering at our actions.
They had so little to laugh about.

A long highway stretches out before me,
Like the gorgeous one in New Mexico
And West Texas.
People say driving there is boring but
It is gorgeous beyond description.
The endless expanse of it all.
Driving through an ancient sea
That disappeared over billions of years.
Where dinosaurs ate whatever the sea left.
Even if the sea only drained in ten thousand years,
It would have happened so slowly that no one saw it.

How far can I see?

Words become true eventually.
Well, the true ones do.
We think we are our thoughts
And our actions.
But we are also words.
First, before anything, we are a word.
We are what we can name,
Not just what we can scold in ourselves.

Before there were words,
Way back then,
Did people dream about dolphins,
As I do every night?
Did our ancestors poop
In front of each other
Like dogs do now?
My dogs look me right in the eye
Only at the moment of poopage,
And never at any other time on their walk.
Were Neanderthal mothers
Embarrassed by their nipples?

If I ask you where God is,
Where would you point?
The spirit, the big God, is
Nowhere we can name.
You would make circular movements
Like the transit of Venus.

The chains we carry but cannot see,
Were handed to us by old German women,
By the Irish, Dutch, Scots,

By the Romanians, Italians, Germans,
The everybody. We are all *everybody*.
All longing for a deeper life.
While we hold the chains.

We lift a veil
On our beginnings and endings.
The shortest glimpse of my life
Is a comforting numbness,

The bondage of sleeplessness
Unless I have written a poem.
Unless I have really listened,
As in deep-down-in-the-real-me listened,
To Mozart or Bach or Handel.
They are the ones who heard me
When I said nothing,
So the least I can do is listen back.

Eternal order.
Detachment always.
The waking coma of mourning
Becomes our morning.
"That was my life,"
I will someday say,
And how will that feel?

God must be totally free.
Isn't that what freedom means,
Being like a god?
Seed and tree are equal miracles,
Part of the grand theater
In the tiny garden of our minds.
What role do we play in the heavens?

Wouldn't Bach be just as beautiful on Jupiter or Mars?
Elusive, mutable, simple, hovering.

The old women, especially the women,
Hover and look at us in the dark.

# One Truth

There is one true poem in the world.
We all can speak our one truth.
And it rhymes only by half.

This is mine:
I am better than I ever thought,
And not nearly as good as I think.

And I am fine like that.
So are you.

Just fucking be kind.
Or at least kinder than you are.

# Polmood Dawn
## For Louisa Stude Sarofim

Well before dawn at Polmood

    Though you'd have to look closely,

    A light comes on.

It is her forever time of day, those hours before the sun,

    When one feels the pulse of the world.

    The day arrives slowly beyond the curtains.

        She is nimble, undistractable,

        Careful, empathic, thoughtful.

The time of day to care about it all is before dawn.

The quotidian, that radical familiar, tells us that memory is habit.

    Spring, Winter, Summer, Fall.

There is a great creative holiness,

An engine we needn't understand.

Nature confers sanctity.

Art has shaped it all.

Agnes Martin's repeated ratios.

Robert Wilson's new ancient scribbles.

Loving thy neighbors

And taking care of them.

There is no diminishing translation of life here.

    There are only the words of "adventuring where marvels be."

Words are to thought as theology is to God.

Only in nature do we see the earth's precious rules.

We curate that which preserves and enlarges.

The gods are here: Janus, Julius, and Augustus still name our months.

Brilliant voices await expansive thoughts, and vice versa.

Language is the voice of all.

      That which we cannot name is not there, for

  Words are their universe.

Summer isn't over,

But a single tree near Roybal has decided on its own that it is autumn.

> Though all of the other trees are green,
>> That *one* tree keeps its own mind,
>
>> And has a sovereignty of generosity.
>
> Much is against custom, but all with high awareness.
>
>> Every tree, every book, every warm piece of art.
>
>> Every bench placed exactly for the sunset.
>
>> The deep red arroyo slicing through grays and greens.
>
> Serenity. Brown thick mud adobe god. Wind.
>
>> Nature is not tamed, just helped.
>
> There is only preserving care.
>
> Those who benefit others at cost to themselves,
>
> Those who practice altruism as a religion,
>
>> They are the true examples.
>
> Dreams of childhood live forever.
>
>> As does gratitude.

## Epilogue

Before dawn at Polmood these things happen:

> The sky turns an eggshell blue.

    Coyotes cackle like teenage girls.

    What you see in the emerging shadows

    Are the ancestors of ancestors,

    Standing guard over the land they tended,

    Land now protected, safe,

    And deeply loved.

She holds ancestors, all of them, in peace,

    Near and far, native and not.

    In the mountain desert,

    A light turns on.

# Paraclete

That which saves us can also harm.
He had a name like Santa Claus.
But his name was pronounced *klous*, like louse,
"Like clouds, but not as pretty," he used to joke.
And we laughed at every joke of his because
Priests were not supposed to be funny.

Children loved him, Father Clauss/rhymes with clouds
And they flocked to him, like a shepherd.
I was one of them.
We were taught that priests were God's proxy,
And when we were taught this, we believed it.
You need to understand that we all believe it.
Belief was our job.

He sat alone in his house in the country.
St. Mary's Road. No one was ever around there.
He had a horse named Savior.
He claimed to love the silence of the countryside.

But his life was not quiet.
None of his fumbles in the dark
All over Southern Indiana,
A place where priests were trusted.
Year after year, people turn to the priests
For everything that is most important.

He met so many children, because he knew how
To draw them towards him. He would embrace and,
Until I was too big, always pick me up and say "hello,"

Drawing me so close to his face I could smell his aftershave.
I liked it when he picked me up.

There was also Mike Allen, who also became a priest.
My brother's best friend in their youthful years.
He picked me up as well, a year longer than anyone else.
He liked boys who were almost but not yet men.
Boys who were not yet stuck where he was,
When he decided to open a door and hide behind it.

The night our father died, in the hospital in Evansville,
Where we did not know anybody, I was the youngest,
The one who had no partner to comfort me,
So I held to Mom, watching a chapter of her life end.
They were all so busy with telling people.
I went to the lobby of the hospital and used the pay phone
To call Father Clauss, the only priest I could think to call.

I said, "Our dad is dying in the next few hours," which
No one else had yet said out loud.
He drove right over. He comforted us.
He was the last person our dad saw in his life.
Extreme unction. Last rites.
His was the last loving face seen by our dad.
In those days they would not let us in to watch him die.

Did I know even then that Father Clauss was a child molester?
His obituary called him "an incurable pedophile."
Is this the stuff of poetry?
No, it certainly is not.
But sometimes only a distillation is real.

There was a retreat, organized by Father Clauss.

1973. I was ten.
We rode horses, and Savior pulled a carriage
"Like in the old days when I was a boy," he said.
Savior pooped on St. Mary's Road.
Father scolded him, "Oh, Savior…how could you?"

We drove in a bus to a high school with a pool,
Which our high school did not have.
We all went swimming and all of the boys
Took their clothes off in front of Father Clauss.

Then we went to a farm where we roasted hot dogs
And marshmallows that we put on the ends of sticks.
"Just like Jesus, Mary, and Joseph on Christmas night,"
He said, giving final prayers. He watched us dress and undress.

He was our Father, our father figure, and just…Father.
We all loved him so very much.
As the fire started to wind down,
Father decided we should all go to bed.
The girls went into the farmhouse but
All of the boys went to the barn with Father Clauss.
There were seminarians with us, I assumed to help out.
I was supposed to sleep next to Brother Martin, and my
Friend Dick Larkin, my best childhood friend, was nearby.
We slept on either side of Brother Martin.

Father Clauss had a favorite boy,
Someone not from our town or parish,
Someone we did not know.
He chose a boy from somewhere distant,
Someone troubled and in need of the kind of love
We were finding and feeling on our retreat.

The favorite boy slept next to Father Clauss
And we all understood: that was *his* boy.
The extraordinary was normalized in Catholicland.
Father Clauss was behind a hay bale with his boy.

I remember feeling the protection of Brother Martin.
I pretended to be asleep so that I could say his name.
"Brother Martin," I would say, sleepily.
Was I trying to seduce him?
Was I jealous that I was not Father Clauss's boy?
Many of us were ten. Clauss's boy was probably fifteen.
What went on that night?

A few years later, there was another retreat.
But this one was bigger, lasting several days
And we were farther from our parents.
It was called Outpost, but it was no outpost.

It was south of us, down by Santa Claus Land
(There's old Santa again in this story)
And just down the road in the other direction
Was Abraham Lincoln's boyhood home.
The log cabin of lore, the candle-making,
The cabin where his mother died.
At the Outpost we felt connected to history.

It was a beautiful camp, full of things
To make children remember it.
Verdant and safe.
You pulled in from the road and just beyond
A small parking lot, you found a screened-in hall.
That is where we ate the food cooked for us by two nuns.

A little further away from the road, on the left,

Was a beautiful lake with a single boat dock.
It felt like a huge lake.
On the side of the lake was the house
Where all of the priests stayed.
Farther up the hill, a hill that felt big,
Were the cabins where all of the boys slept.
Four to a cabin.
There was a single outhouse
Where the older boys said snakes lurked.

Again, swimming.
The day after we arrived
We went to Lincoln State Park.
To the big lake where we all swam
And then we went to the showers
Where Father Mark took his clothes off.
And we all marveled at his beautiful body
Though we did not know we were marveling.
He lingered in the shower for as long as he could.
Naked. Swinging around.
He was hairy where we had none.

Later, back at the Outpost.
Late at night, after dinner, campfire, and prayers.
A boy and I decided to take a boat out
Into the middle of the huge lake
So that we could kiss.
We were ashamed and scared to kiss
In the woods or anywhere near the cabins.
Because we did not want the other boys to see us.
And we were silently, always unspoken, afraid
Of the priests, of Father Mark, and Mike Allen,
And Father Clauss, who showed up for one night only.
Like a nightclub entertainer.

Was he there with his boy?
Did I somehow know even on that night
That he would someday minister to our dad
At the moment he passed out of life?

I read that Father Clauss died in New Mexico
At the Servants of the Paraclete
The fancy name for the home for abusers.
It was a prison, to be sure, but a nice one,
Where priests who harmed boys could be safe
The *cura animarum*
But where was the New Mexico retreat
For the boys they brought to orgasm
Before they knew what orgasms were?
Who will heal their wounds until the end of life?

# Lucienne Boyer Sings "Parlez-moi d'amor"

Are there songs you listen to every day?
I want a world that never gets tired of songs.
I could hear Lucienne Boyer sing this song
Every day for the rest of my life
And beyond.

She makes me think
Of Paris, of the best of romance,
Of the pain of being in love,
And the sweetness.
Of Montmartre,
Of my déjà vu
When I once turned
To descend a stairway.
The famous one
That is in all the photos.

My friends thought
I was having an episode,
Maybe even a stroke.
I was in a panic at
The top of the stairs.

I saw it all before me.
I was a woman in 1930
The year that Lucienne Boyer
Recorded *Parlez-moi d'amour.*
I was thrown down the stairs

By a jealous man who would
Never allow me to live after
I told him I could not be with him.

I felt invisible hands.
Hands at the end of
Two very strong arms
Which had held and caressed,
Yet now were pushing me
To my death in Paris.

I felt my neck break
Shortly after my fall.
And I could hear the scream
Of the woman who found me
And the sadness in the voice
Of the policeman who
Pronounced me dead.

Tell me about love.
About tender things.
Cradle me in words
That you caress with
The sweetest voice.

The little music box
In the background
Of the most beautiful song.
Then a cello and violin.
The most romantic waltz

*Parlez-moi d'amour*
*Redites-moi des choses tendres*

Smiling with tears in the eyes.
I could hear it every day.

# Pat Robertson's Heaven

Pat Robertson assumed he went to heaven.
His little perfect white puffy-cloud heaven,
Where white people did not have to be reminded
Of all of the evil they had done in the name of Jesus.

It is a terrible feeling, like that song about Mr. Karp
In the gay gay gay gay gay musical, *A Chorus Line*,
To feel nothing when a person dies, and even worse
To feel some degree of delight that his idiocy is gone.

But Pat Robertson died, finally, and I felt no glee.
I felt no sadness either, for his hateful small mind.
Because death is the great secret that people like him
Need you to believe that he knows. Indeed, that *only* he
Knows this secret. Because if you believe this, you will
Keep sending him money, and then he can keep his
Hate-filled, stupid, puny, fear-mongering television show.

A life mired in words
He didn't understand
Used to hate those he didn't love
To make money from those
He could control.
This earthquake was caused by this
Nonsense.
This hurricane was cause by sodomy.
Nonsense.
What a waste of what might have been.
A waste of the few hundred thousand hours
Which are our real blessings in this life.

Do not reach the end of your life
And have people remember the things
You did to create more hate in the world.
This man deserves no heaven
For the hell he created here.
But I'm sure he is there anyway
Because the world is better than anything
His tiny scared thoughts could create.
Roast in peace, you venal asshole.
And fuck you for making me think
Such a horrible thought about anyone.

# Photo of Our Parents, November 22, 1941

Eighteen years before I was born.
There they are in this photo.
My dad is singing.
"I want a girl
Just like the girl
That married dear old dad!"
Or one of those great old songs.
Mom looks embarrassed.
Between them is Aunt Jenny, huge smile.
Aunt Virginia, who less than thirty years later died young
Of lung cancer. She could never stop smoking.

I remember being at her house.
She and Uncle Don were our parents' closest friends.
Uncle Don must have taken the picture of
Their wedding day, or he would have been in it.
They had no money to hire a photographer.
But we went to visit her, and I sat on her lap.
She was so frail, and I pulled out a candy cigarette.
Children my age had candy cigarettes.
Can you imagine?
We would pretend to smoke.

Aunt Ginny. She was Virginia and some people
Spelled her Jenny, while for others she was Ginny.
I was sitting on her lap pretending to smoke.
She pulled it out of my hand
And threw it across the room.

But on that day, the day of the photo,
Surrounded by winter trees,
They were all so young and happy.
It was a Saturday, that November 22, 1941
They had a honeymoon night in Jasper at
What felt like a fancy hotel.
They had a breakfast the next morning
And went back home to start their lives.

But only two weeks later, on Sunday
The 7th of December, a new world
Asserted itself, and the photo taken just
A few hundred hours before would never
Be taken again.

# Phra Alack

Shall we fly on a bright cloud of music?

The smallest and least important role in
Any famous play must be Phra Alack in
*The King and I*.
You don't remember him?
Hardly surprising.

He comes on the boat after the first song
With the Kralahome, the sort-of Prime Minister
And he asks Anna,
Missus Anna Leonowens,
The teacher of royal schoolchildren,
A few questions before he gets kicked.

The director said we had to look more
Siamese so, "get a tan."
But we could not get *that* tanned.
So we all wore dark makeup all over
Our skin. It smelled of the beach.
And it was all over everything for months.

I was fourteen years old
In that summer of 1978,
That summer of *The King and I*,
Well, the summer of *our King and I*.
It had been twenty-seven years
After the musical had taken the world,
And been made into a famous movie.
So the show was very young,

Like us all.

That was forty-five years ago now,
That summer of 1978,
So the musical is now
Seventy-two years old.
How many of the original
Royal children are still living?
"Getting to Know You."
The show will be older by
The time you read this sentence.

It was the first time I
Understood what magic
Could feel like, what theater
Meant and felt and held in trust.

I read the script constantly, playing every role.
I read every stage direction.
I played the songs constantly,
Just me at the piano, singing Anna's
Long monologue scene,
"Shall I Tell You What I Think of You?"
I had a way to perform every line.

It did not matter
How good we were
Or were not.
Being good was not the point of doing it.
It was summer in southern Indiana.
They were years of romance,
Of joining the river of the world.
Late at night, after rehearsal,
We would go to the only restaurant

That stayed open and we would have
Burgers and feel like we were very New York.

We had parties out at the Capehart Lodge
Out on a farm, built for parties.
We all drank so much.
And the laughter was immense.
People fell in what felt like love.
Not with people
But with the feeling of that summer.
We never wanted it to end.

My character's name did not sit easily
In Hoosier mouths.
Phra Alack always sounded like "frolic."
Once, fascinated with the script,
I was standing off stage right
(I had just learned that stage right was on the left)
Following along. Suddenly, there was silence.
The script said "Phra Alack."
That was me.
I had missed the entire cue.

The King and Anna, onstage,
Needed interrupting.
And I left them high and dry.
"Where the HELL is Phra Alack?"
The King said, sounding more
Like the actor than the King of Siam.
I scurried out the to the stage and
Blurted out my line.
And that was the merciful end
Of my life as an actor.

In these dreams I've loved you so
That by now I think I know.

# Playing House

Most children play house.
Boys and girls both.
I used to play house with ants.
Real ones.
I would find an anthill in our yard and
Imagine I was the mom of a big family.
Always mom, never dad.
All of the other ants worked for our big family.
We were in charge.
I was the mom.

Every day, one of my sons would
Be plagued with some terrible tragedy.
All of my other children, many of them
Would gather around me and comfort me.
I would cry for hours.
Even as a little boy there was
Always an old woman inside me.

I would turn over the dirt
With a stick, as little boys do,
And look at all of the scurrying energy.
They would go mad with industry after
I had destroyed their home,
Exposed it to a light it had never seen.
They were hard at work before,
But after I destroyed their house,
After they got over the shock,
They would go right back to business
As though nothing had happened.

They would rebuild instantly.
By the next day, every time,
Their homes looked like I had done nothing.

Then, every few weeks,
And I am still ashamed of this.
I would get the gasoline tank from the garage,
The one Dad used for the mower,
Open an anthill, and douse them with it.

They would have their usual terror
But I made it worse by pouring poison over them.
Then I would set it on fire and watch them burn.
Their frail little bodies would crumple and wilt.
And then I would cry because I was sad.

How could I be so cruel? And why?
It is not something I could do now.
But children must need to test their cruelty.
All children have this possibility of cruelty.
Why do some never leave it behind them?

# Playing in the Rain

Before I was five,
So still in the '60s,
I played in the rain.

Do all children do this?
I suppose they do.
Playing in the rain.

After the hardest rain
I had ever seen,
I went across the street.

It was a torrent.
We lived on a slight incline.
So the water was roaring

Left to right.
I made boats out of sticks
So I could follow them.

Down the block,
Then down the next block,
Then into a stream

That went under a bridge
Under the highway.
Towards a bigger stream.

I knew the bigger stream
So I could picture it all.

The streams collecting ever more.

I went to the map
To find the names of the stream.
And to discover

That the stream emptied
Into the White River
Which wasn't white, but brown.

And from there to the Wabash
To the Ohio
To the Mississippi

To the Gulf and on
To the rest of the world.
My little boats

That I made out of sticks
Could sail the whole world
But I might never know.

So imagine the world
That I could imagine
From just one rain.

# Looking at Potsdam from the Train

Churchill, Truman, Stalin
In their comfy chairs at Cecilienhof.
It is the photo of Potsdam we all know.
From the train, one sees the beautiful lakes.

It is a suburb of Berlin,
One of places that survived
The onslaught, allowing the leaders
To meet there weeks after the war.

Now it is a calm and sweet
Place for weekenders from the capital.
Just what it should have been all along.

What did Churchill think of the place?
He was replaced as Prime Minister
During the conference, so he left.

Would we have had the Cold War
At all if Churchill had stayed?
All the beautiful homes around the lake,
Do they all know what happened here?

And then the train left and I stopped
Thinking about Potsdam. People fall in love
There, every day, and have big huge lives
About which we know nothing.

# Presence

Often.
Several times a day.
I must remind myself
Not only where,
But *who* I am.

Does this happen to everyone?
Do others hear themselves
Speaking or teaching or making music
And have to remind themselves
Of exactly who they are?

Is this how we know of being?
Do we reach a summit after which
We realize that we are realizing?
When we recognize our self, not as *us*,
But as something else entire?

When I say "I am thinking,"
I am expressing the oldest primal
Urges of the world, the fires that fuel
The earthquakes and the wind and the
Long deep time that knows it is time.

The most beautiful thing I know
Is that I thought of knowing it.
I stare into knowingness,
And remind myself who I am.
But it must be reminded.
It does not know on its own.

This is such a consistent theme
Of every moment of my life.
Like that night when I was ten
And Dad drove me home from
Vincennes, and I had my own
Steering wheel, a little toy one.
Already steering my course
As my dad actually drove.

I still do not know, half a century later,
Who was speaking on that night.
As we drove the almost-hour,
The day was exhausting itself.
The sun was behind us,
Still lighting California
While it cast shadows on us.

For those fifty-sixty minutes,
I outlined my entire life to my dad.
And when I think back on that drive,
My life has been exactly as I told him.
How did I know?

For it was not me speaking.
I spoke about the Dreyfus Affair
And Queen Victoria,
And Verdi and Mozart,
And *All in the Family*,
And Maude, and abortion,
And all sorts of things about which
I knew absolutely nothing.

I told him I wanted to learn

All about Shakespeare.
He stared at me, eyes off the road.
I was ten. I knew nothing of this at all.
Who was speaking to my shocked parent?
For it was not his son. It was not me.

# Red Speedo

The play about the swimmer in the red Speedo.
Everyone goes to watch the boy in the title role,
Pretending we are watching the play.

Then you are surprised that the play is really good.
Playing with huge issues in small ways.
Funny, serious, and seriously funny.

Unmasking our competitiveness.
Exposing our corroding masculine breaths.
Winking at our hypocrisy.
Noticing our obsessions that linger
Always on the surface of the pool.

What do we enhance, and why?
What is fair help and what isn't?
A great playwright is the real poet of the world.

People writing great plays go unnoticed now.
Unfamous. Un-talked-about. Uncontroversial.

Don't we want a world that goes to plays,
And gets pissed off by them,
And protests them,
And cries at them,
And lets them quietly change the world?

# Standing on the San Andreas

I started a novel here.
On this bay named after a bodega
Who names a bay after a grocery?

Standing on the south side
of Bodega Head, peering towards
Point Reyes just at the right time of day

The sun setting, but not for an hour,
I am standing on the Pacific plate.
Just across the bay is the North American.

I am standing on one continent
And looking at another.
But it is all just California.

It is a place of unearthly beauty
And of unearthly danger.
Standing on the San Andreas

It could snap at any moment.
Or it could snap in one million years.
No one knows, not even a god.

Because the plates move.
They just…move.
We don't get to know why.

But can we never lose the wonder,
That I can stand on Bodega Head
And see nature's elemental force?

Lear stood on a cliff like this.
So did Gloucester, blinded.
But this cliff is different.

This cliff used to be near Mexico.
It is on the left side of California
And it is not where it used to be.

Neither am I.
My tectonic plates
Have shifted beneath me.

# Sausalito Summer, 1968

Sea water and sluice.
The houseboat at the Waldo Point piers
Had a singular scent.
There was nothing in the world like it.

It was more than just the everywhere ocean.
It smelled of the '60s, a world coming apart,
With beautiful remnants of worlds rapidly passing.

The supper club of the Spinnaker was just over there
Where you could still see ladies in hats.
But flower children were not only
In Haight-Ashbury. They were everywhere,
And the ladies in hats hated them like they were insects.

Sausalito had a scent of lichen and
Tunicates and coral in those years,
And no small amount of gasoline
Fueling the boats. Petrol and sea water.
Somewhere, not far away,
A fish was being grilled.
Does plankton have a scent?
I heard that the open ocean, far from shore,
Has no odor. It is only the plankton
And the wedding of the shore to the sea
That causes any smells. Is that true?
All of it combined to smell like
Only old Sausalito could smell.

The wooden slats and ropes on

Old pilings, swaying with the tide.
Quays, docks, piers, jetties. Wharves…
All have different origins and meanings
In the world but they are
Interchangeable in Sausalito.
Strange.
The words seem to have more to do with
Who is saying them,
More than what they describe.

1968 was the first time I heard the words
Ecosystem or gnarly.
That's boss. Outta sight, baby.
Life was language then,
For there was nothing else,

Not in my little five-year-old life.
The war generation was old but
Not as old as I am now.
Groovy. Righteous.
Bread meant money;
Now it just means bread.

My birthday party at Alta Mira was a gas.
Now gas is just gas.
If we ate fast, we scarfed.
Neato. Grody.
*Sock it to me*
In fast repeated sixteenth notes.

Tremors.
Somehow the adults knew
There was an earthquake but

On the houseboat it felt like nothing
But a different kind of rocking.

The engine of belief,
The inner motor of the world,
Made California so beautiful.
Sausalito looks so much itself
Because of the power of the earth
That not even the weakness of men
Could change or fully destroy.

Life was free and open that summer
I was so much more loveable then.
Who could imagine a little boy like me,
The little boy I was that summer,
Would or could grow up anything but blissful?

The yellow beetle, the Volkswagen, the Nazi car,
Though nobody in Sausalito talked about Nazis.
Not even our dad, who had looked them in the face
Only twenty-five years before.
He shot them, but he did not
Mind one of his sons owning a Nazi car.
He did not even think about it.
In 1968 it was the slug-bug, the Herbie.
Helen Hayes in my favorite movie that
We saw at Lake Tahoe in that same summer.

Julie Christie was there, though I don't know why.
Was she living with someone on a houseboat?
I didn't know her but all of the adults
Kept talking about her, whispering when
They thought I was asleep.

She was beautiful, and she spoke to me
One time out on the dock, or was it
The jetty?
"Such a cutie," she said,
Stroking my long blond hair.
Her touch was so gentle that
I sometimes still tear up
When I remember it.

And there was a wrecked show boat,
Paddle wheel and all, on the shore.
It hadn't seen water in years.
What was it doing there?
Had Waldo Point put it there on purpose?

Deer came down to the shoreline.
There was a freeway even then,
So I don't know how they got there.
Where did they go during the day?
How were there not dead deer on the 101?
I am told they don't go to the bay any longer.
When was the sad last day when
They stopped going all the way to the bay?

The fog whisked silently over the hills
More often that it does now.
The air has changed since that long-ago summer.

Crossing the Golden Gate Bridge now
Coming from the city.
You still go through the tunnel,
Slipping into Northern California in a few seconds.
People still honk in the tunnels,
Like kids do in haunted houses at state fairs.

But there is nothing in the mess of love
And life that is *now*, more than half a century
Further on, that makes me miss life more.
I long for it rather than remembering it,
Because it was a feeling, a newness,
A time when nothing was degraded,
Even while the world seemed to fall apart.

Was it falling apart, or just falling into itself?
The world was less armored then, less embracing
Of cynics. Men had fought wars to be real,
So they would allow themselves anything but gratitude.

Sausalito had that scent of freedom and possibility.
There was no need to pray because the air was sacred.
The pure simple smell of it all was life remembering us.

We ferried our hours over the water that held
No dangers for us that summer. Still, in this time of
So much change, I am transported with that memory.
Age rested in the piers that summer
As it sits now in our bones.

# Unfinished Symphony

Franz Schubert sat in a coffee house in Vienna
Just off Stephansplatz, just like some of the cafés
That are there still. A lost world lingers.

On a day like this one, blue and cool,
Ludwig van Beethoven entered the café,
Just as Franz had hoped he would.

Franz, everyone called him Franz,
Was frozen in his chair, his hands grasping
A cup of steaming chocolate coffee that
Smelled of cocoa and sugar and youth.

Frozen not from cold,
But from the sight of
Ludwig across the café,
Franz wanted more than
Anything he had ever felt
To approach him.

He wanted to shake his hand
To look into his eyes
To hear the tone of his voice
To find some secret of the madness
That came from his quill.

Sounds that Franz heard in
Candlelit rooms that smelled of flowers
Where quartets and trios played
And even the big impossible symphonies

That sounded to Franz like traveling through
The cosmos.

All of that desire sat in the air between them
In a single café in Vienna, near Stephansdom
Where Ludwig read some broadsheets
And wrote some letters while he, too,
Enjoyed his cocoa and pastry.

Franz sat and stared at him
Watching every tic and movement
Looking for any clue to any secret
That might unlock something within him.

The symphony that Franz could not finish
The endless beautiful rolling melody of it
Still sits in that café
In the air between Ludwig and Franz.
If you are quiet you can hear it
Through the clinking of the glasses.

# The Line

The wasting of so much time.
But, is it?
Screaming at strangers
On the mysterious line,
The invisible space in which
Which we all now live.
Where, exactly, *is* the line we are on?

It keeps us, I hope,
From screaming at real people,
The people we know and love.

And it helps, I know,
Even for a moment in the morning,
To just say what one wants to say about
The ludicrous,
Stupid, mean, boring, uninformed,
Small, bigoted, racist, homophobic,
Sexist, misogynist, reductionist, frustrating
Nonsense that people spout.

But who does it help?
No one is listening.

# Semele

Semele, rhymes with Emily
Juno, rhymes with you know.
Trees where you sit
Shall crowd into a shade.

Music's sensuous joys
We feel through Handelian surprises
Easing life's noise,
With what emotion emphasizes.

Lakes of Maotia, Scythian Hills.
Whatever the spirit wills,
In the mirror of the dragon's eye
The horrifying chills supply.

Behold! Auspicious flashes rise,
Our ears and expectation flies.
The grateful odor swift ascends
To hear the rhyme of image bends.

Luck omens bless our rites
Handel days and scary night.
Sure success will crown your love
So few words will rhyme above.

On this auspicious day
Invent no new delay
Guide me towards the joyful *wants*
Upon a time, they said but once.

# Simple Elegy

American thoughts that linger in Europe:
You will not realize for at least seventy-two hours,
As you walk around, as I did, Kensington Gardens,
Or the gorgeous Tiergarten in Berlin,
Or the Prater in Vienna.
Or, indeed, anywhere.
Finally, it dawns on you.

You realize that for several consecutive minutes,
You have not thought about getting shot.

# Time

In the most distant time, before poetry,
Even before words, how was life?
The sky, surely, was then blue,
And it was noticed, by someone,
That birds sang.

Were there actions before words?
They must have called each other something.
And they must have cried when they were betrayed.
Surely, not every moment was just survival.

There must have been little pockets of time
In the long days of our ancestors.
Not the ones we know, but
Going back forty, fifty thousand years,
Back on the savannas and in the caves.
And in the small huts they must have built.

Moments when they understood they were alive
And under a sky
And under a canopy of trees.
The sun still rose and set.
They must have noticed it.

They were not only our ancestors.
Their young new words had ancestors.
We will never know them.
But we know them.

# A Toilet in Berlin

It was not

The most embarrassing thing ever.

But it was close.

Do you want to know the *most* embarrassing?

Of course you do.

The most embarrassing thing ever

Was not in a toilet, but in the lobby of the

Sydney Opera House.

Yes, that one. The famous one. The sails.

A soprano raced up to me with a glass of champagne.

I had just conducted a performance.

"Maestro, I'm so eager to work with you!

"My name so easy to remember! 'Shu.'"

(Pointing to her shoe.)

"Chin"

(Pointing to her chin.)

And then it happened, the moment I regret forever.

I still do not know why, but I said, out of character:

"Wow, it's a good thing your name isn't shit head."

I had not thought of the most awful thing I said

In so many years.

Because

I hate thinking about it.

It embarrasses me all over again.

But recently, I ran to a toilet for

Intermission of an

Opera in

Berlin.

Germans have funny small toilets tucked away all over

The place.

I found one.

Locked the door.

Did my thing.   Except.

At the crucial moment, I found out that I

Had *not* locked the door.

A woman tore through the door so fast that there was no hiding.

She screamed, "*Scheissekopf!!!*"

*Shit. Head.*

I had been repaid in full.

# Trost

I was about four,
Playing with a truck in our ditch
Very hot weather.
The man across the street,
Reverend Trost,
Was pushing his lawn mower.
He was the Methodist minister,
Like the one in *Our Town*.

He'd waved at me when he started mowing.
Full sun. It was hot and humid.
Indiana summer. I was in the shade.
Occupied with my truck, making little hills.
I noticed that the mower stopped moving.
He was on the ground.
I knew something was wrong
But I was too young to know what.

I ran in to tell Mom.
She called an ambulance.
Everyone in the neighborhood
Came to our lawn and stood around.
We all watched the men carry him away.
"He's already gone," several people said.
"Gone where?" I asked, not understanding.
"I'm sure he had a heart attack," someone else said.
"No!" I insisted. "No one attacked him!" I said,
Understanding even less than I thought.

Not more than an hour later

Someone came to say he was dead.
"Was gone before he hit the ground,"
They said.
I was the last person he saw on earth.
Did he wave at me?
In memory I think he did.

It was only years later that I realized
The weight of what I had witnessed.
The end of a man's life.
As I got older, I learned that *Trost*
Meant *vow*. He was Reverend Vow.
A promise.

I saw this man's life end.
So I made a promise, too.
I wonder if I have kept it.

# Vienna Moment

The ones you are supposed to flirt with
Whether or not you ever meet them,
Will always return to your field
More than once.

I first saw him out in Stephansplatz.
When he smiled.
Then I saw him at Doblinger,
The famous music store.
Ah, a musician, I thought.

We flirted to the point of
Just dropping into a doorway
And kissing for many minutes.
I felt him get hard,
But we could go no further.

No names, no numbers,
No hotel addresses.
Nothing.
Just that passionate kissing
In a doorway of an antique store
That was thankfully closed
Because those shops never
Seem to be open.

I got to the opera that night.
*Die Walküre*, the great Valkyrie herself,
And there he was, up in the standing room,
With his boyfriend, who obviously had no idea

That his guy had been kissing me that afternoon.

Every intermission, we stared each other down.
Smiling. Knowing. Wanting more than we had time to do.
I never knew his name, and by the fifth hour of the opera,
I had no way of knowing where he was staying.

We watched each other leave,
As the great and the good dispersed
Into the Vienna night.
He said something to his boyfriend.
And kissed him good night.
"I want to take a walk,"
I was close enough to hear him say.

He did want to take a walk.
A thousand feet behind me.
All the way to the Beethoven,
The hotel named after the man himself.
The man who would not approve
Of what I did for the next several hours.
Ode to joy, indeed.

# Walking in Kensington Gardens

When I broke my knee
That distant stormy night
In Santa Fe, many years ago now.
I was walking down Agua Fria
When my left leg collapsed.
Quadriceps tendon severed.

A woman came from nowhere.
An angel named Leticia.
I never saw her before or after.
She was there for that moment
While I waited for the ambulance,
And a storm was brewing.
Leticia told me everything was
Going to be fine, "but you are quite injured."

I told her, from nowhere,
That I had only one real fear:
That I would not be able to take
A long walk in Kensington Gardens again,
One of my favorite things in the world.

"I assure you," Leticia said.
"You will walk as much as you want
In Kensington Gardens…
After you learn to walk again."
I cried. She already knew what
I was facing, long before I did.

And she was right. I learned to walk all over.
And now many times I have walked the
Gorgeous pathways of Kensington Gardens,
Leading into Hyde Park and the Serpentine.
The sight of the Crystal Palace,
The home of the Horse Guards.

It is my favorite walk in the world,
From somewhere in Kensington,
Where I've been so often gifted to stay,
And I pass into the Gardens right at the
Famous palace, the home of Diana, Margaret,
And the birthplace of Queen Victoria,
Where everyone now takes their selfie.

London's lungs, where each age
Takes their walk for different reasons.
Some reaching destinations.
Some relaxing.
That old man there, on the bench
That looks like the bench at the end of
*Finding Neverland*, the scene with that
Amazing child actor.
That man is sitting on the bench and
Thinking about his late wife, the woman
With whom he went to the park all the time.
Where they talked about Shakespeare they had
Seen at the Old Vic with Olivier and Smith.

There's that woman with her caretaker,
Taking in the same beautiful June day
That I am, but she has had at least thirty
More June days than I have had.

The flower walk. The Albert Memorial.
Always remembering Mark Twain's famous
Takedown of it, assuming from afar that it must
Be Jesus, instead of the unelected
Foreign husband of a monarch.

I have walked Kensington to West End
So very many times now, that I have my
Signposts that I watch for, like old friends.
Certain benches, though I never sit on them.
Memories of Princess Diana, whom I once saw
Jogging in the park. Reading about the Crystal
Palace, the most exciting place of its time.

And always, always, are the flowers, surely
Among the world's most beautiful plantings.
And the places in the park that are still wild,
Where kings and princes might still hunt deer.

Every person who has ever lived in London
For centuries now, has walked the gardens.
Nazi pilots knew every feature of the park
And used the great corners as signposts
To be sure they bombed the right palace.

# On Waterloo Bridge

Not so very long ago
Less than a decade.
I was proposed to on this bridge.
The man I'd chosen to spend life with.
Surprised me in London on Waterloo Bridge.
It was a moment of supreme happiness.

It has always been my favorite London spot.
Because it is the view of views of the great city.
St. Paul's, gleaming in the distance, with the
Spires of the City competing for its attention.
Big Ben, of course, and the ugly garish Ferris.
The Houses of Parliament. Westminster.
The view of views, the greatest city.

Famous from movies, but more famous for
What you can see from it. Vivien Leigh, forever.

The sweetest man on earth, the wounded one,
Wanted to propose to me on Waterloo Bridge
Because he knew what it would mean to me,
For the rest of my life, to have that memory.
He went to enormous lengths to create that romance.

Now, not so very many years later,
I have crossed Waterloo Bridge again,
Several times. The first time was very hard,
But I did not shed the tears I expected.

There was a time I did not know this man.

We were strangers
To each other
Until we weren't.
Now, we are strangers again,
Having shared so many important moments,
Moments that led us to this bridge.

But the bridge stands, as beautiful as ever.
It has seen thousands of lovers come and go.
It knows that the river beneath it flows on,
Uncaring about whoever walks across.

I will always love Waterloo Bridge,
And I treasure that brief moment with him,
Grateful to have known that instant of
Real joy, pure and overwhelming.
It will always be ours.
We must hold the joys we touch,
Even while they do not last.

# Winter Trees

One of my favorite things
And one of the most beautiful
All over the world
Is the sight of trees in winter.

Their great arteries stretching to the sky.
The gray overcast beauty
Behind their lacy black veins.

They are more unique, even, than we are.
No two views are the same.
They are mirroring the solar system, surely.
Or maybe they are the enlargement of the
Gates and alleys inside us all.

Somewhere back in deep time
As the earth cooled and life imagined itself,
Which we know is what happened,
The trees were noticed.

The world is too random to imagine
Anything else, or to let people have their illusions.
The world is cold, taking the leaves.
But somehow the tree holds within itself
The heat for new leaves.

Somewhere back in deep time,
The veins of everything larger than us
Became the veins of trees
Reaching back towards the heavens

From where they came.
For millions of years before us
There was the canopy,
Season after season.
A billion times a billion leaves.
They made the world hospitable to us.

I have been all over the world in winter.
Australia, Russia, England, Canada, America.
And though their trees are all very different.
In the winter they share the great skeleton
Of the trees, the winter trees.
One of the world's beautiful things.

# Thirty-six one-word poems that happen each day

Quiescent

Translucent

Enamor

Mellifluous

Dolor

Paroxysm

Resplendent

Luxuriate

Frolic

Ensorcell

Conniption

Murmuration

Ejaculate

Wax

Lithe

Exhilarate

Jocundity

Majesty

Blithesomeness

Ennoble

Gossamer

Transcendency

Eminence

Invigilate

Yare

Micturition

Supine

Petrichor

Aurora

Labyrinthine

Diaphanous

Sibilance

Lagniappe

Epiphany

Panacea

Abyssopelagic

# Wreckers

Wreckers away.
Tales of people who wreck ships.
The lore of God's justice and
Nature's plunder.
Reminders of those all around us
Who have no problem wrecking lives.

I never thought I would know men who
Would sleep with the wives of their friends,
Wrecking households who had supported him.
Who accused *others* of lying while he did.

The leeches and Bradleys and Bens and this
Guy and that guy and that hot one and that one, too
They are all the same person unknown to each other.
Preying on wounded happiness,
Finding the most vulnerable point
At which they can sting and feel what, exactly?
Power. Control.
Some security over their insecurity.
Searching for Mommy's love in
Occupied arms, or avenging Mommy's neglect.

You are supposed to care about people.
Your soulmate does not put you through hell.
Chaos is not love. Complications are not a sign
Of life and care and support and newness.
What happened to the enormous
Care we felt for each other?

Old patterns. Choruses of wreckers
Wreaking their havoc around the world.
Accusing others of what they do themselves.
Where is the responsibility for our care?

Telling themselves lies,
Invoking God where
God is most absent.

Condemned to the sea for
Lighting fires that might save lives.
We are taught to fear the witches
Instead of the people who burned them.
The sea consumes us.

# Hearing the Brahms Second Symphony for the First Time

A memory of my brother.
California coast.
A powdered calm sea.
His house near Mussel Rock.
Where the great trauma
Erupted in the earth in 1906.

I was alone in the house.
I had listened to nothing but
*Fidelio* for day after day.
On his nice record player
Sitting on the beautiful
California blue carpeting.

The record was right there.
And I had heard Tony,
My dear late brother,
Mention the beauty of Brahms.

I can still see the distant fog
Hours off the coast,
Fighting with the sun.

I found the first movement
Old worldish, though I did not
Know what that meant.

But then the moment came.
A few seconds into the second movement.
The miracle. The most staggering
Music I had ever heard, until that moment.

Whenever I conjure it my mind's ear,
Which is at least once a day,
I am astounded. I still am.
The most beautiful few moments
Of any work of music.
How is it possible?
How can this music exist in
The same place of such pain?
It is too beautiful to be true.

# United Methodist Church, Washington, Indiana, 1979

It was the end of the '70s,
So who knows what happened?
I was sixteen, so not old enough to
*Really* know what I was seeing.

I was early for a rehearsal for a play
That was in one of their many rooms.
The church is huge, or it felt huge
To a sixteen-year-old.

I have the feeling that
If I saw the church today
I would think that it is
Actually quite small.

But I walked into the part
Of the church where there
Was an office behind a big
Window, and a lady at a desk.

I did not know the lady
But I always knew she
Was there, and had seen her.
But I did not know her name.

When any of us from the theater
Would enter the church, she would
Totally ignore us, which did not bother

Anyone. We thought it was very funny.

But on that day when I walked in,
I glanced through the window
To her desk, not to say hello,
But just to see her there.

She was sitting there, typing,
But her head, for just an instant,
Was not human. She was a frog.
But her frog's head was huge.

I was petrified. Truly, it was
The moment of my life when
I felt the most terror. And in
My memory, I might have screamed.

Because when I looked away,
Like turning away from a dead
Animal in the road, I tried to collect
Myself and move along.

But when I looked at her again,
She looked at me with her real head.
She was no longer a frog.
And she smiled and waved.

# Nilo Cruz in Aspen

I was not starstruck.
I do not get starstruck.
Except that time when I
Met Olivia de Havilland.
And even then, I was just
Speechless; I didn't say anything.

But with Nilo, I was seeing a poet.
I saw the poet first, then I saw the man.
And the man is the poem and
The poet is the man. He is both.
I have only one real talent in life;
Recognizing the beauty of other men.

But with Nilo, I saw a beauty in myself
Simply by looking at him. His eyes caught
Mine several times, each more beautiful than
The last. I could gaze into his eyes forever
And never twice see the same man.

I am wounded, possibly forever,
By a love that could only wound.
But now I wonder if maybe I could,
Again, at least feel the slightest feeling
Of love and trust and youth for someone.

I do not know this man, so I only know
That just as the wounds I have
Felt are my own; they were not imposed
Without my permission. I invited them.

But with Nilo, what I am seeing is a long
Night of poetry, in his eyes and smile, and
In the pain which is chiseled into his
Gorgeously handsome face.

I have seen a lot of beauty
In my life, but, it is true that
I have never seen more beautiful eyes
Than I did last night. He is all heat
And moisture and poetry and life.
My mind is a blizzard today.
He will probably never know
Until he reads this, if he does.

# Strasbourg Cathedral, 2001

I had grand plans of loving Strasbourg
When I went there to work in November
Of 2001, just months after the worst September.

Tensions were high. It rained without cease.
Gray, cold, dismal, with early sunsets. Swimming.
When I finally figured out their silly rules.
That had all the French bureaucracy combined
With German nitpickiness. Just to swim. Jesus.

I was both lonely and alone. Bored and trying.
Trying to do anything to keep from being lonely.
Visiting a sex house several times too often.
Meeting a guy who worked in the music store,
But who pretended not to know me when I came in.

The work was difficult.
Poor cast, mostly, and an
Over-interpreting director.

And little did I know that it was to be
The last few weeks of my mother's life.
That only became known later, in December.

But in those early weeks of November,
I noticed I was being followed late at night.
By groups of men speaking in Farsi and French.
Especially along Quai de Paris and Quai Desaix.

One night, particularly late and dark,
Four followed me closely, and as I entered
My apartment building, an outer door that led
To an inner door, they said something about Allah.
And in French, something about death, specifically
Death to faggots from America. That would be me.

I called the police, who came right over.
But they thought I was being hysterical.
And "typical for an American after 9/11."
And I told my employers about it all.
They also laughed at my paranoia.
So, I looked over my shoulder
More and more, and went to work.

Three days later, huge news.
The French police had thwarted
A terrorist attack that was to blow up
Strasbourg Cathedral and take hostages
At the European Parliament.
Several photos were published,
And two of the men were the ones
Who followed me.
Was I paranoid?

# Thoughts During
# *Das Lied von der Erde*

It is too beautiful
And much too much.

Trying to understand the world
With grand gestures that mirror it.
But which feels inadequate as anything
Except extravagance.

Isn't it music for musicians?
What does an audience take away
From such indulgences as a drinking
Song about apes that drowns out the tenor?

The music is otherworldly beautiful.
It makes you ache with itself, not with
Its images, which are enough on their own.

The sunburst of love has been copied
By many composers, but is never so
Very beautiful as when it is by Mahler.
In Aspen, the breeze began to stir
As if hearing the music up in the hills.

Horn calls, oboes, glassy vibrations
Ignite the air and bring a mirror for sex
To all the youngsters who haven't figured
Out themselves, much less the vastness of
Nature itself. One can see Mahler sitting in

His cabin in the Dolomites, freed from all
Of the pressures his talent placed on him.

It is so beautiful that it makes you feel
He could have written three more symphonies
Just out of these poems, sitting in the mountains
Where he could be happy, trying to convey
Feelings about feelings,
Conflicting simplicities.
Impossible possibilities.
The light shifted and another
Phrase took shape into itself.

The song about the handsome boys
Was played by a bunch of handsome bass boys.
The spot where Christa Ludwig fought with
Leonard Bernstein in Israel, concerns of hers
That he totally ignored and played down in front
Of the orchestra, as he did what he wanted.
We do not do controversies about such things now.

When Mahler was alive, even with
All of the terrible difficulties,
There was a meta-feeling,
True or not, that we could do anything,
That large things were possible.

That is why we must perform *Das Lied* now,
To be sure that we still know that big ideas are
Possible, and not only possible, desirable.
Life is little things, but we only move forward
From the people who do not follow rules.
From the ones who dream big and have unruly

Minds and misbehave sometimes and who
Are maddening and exasperating.

*Das Lied* always makes me think
Of the "great" earthquake in San Francisco
Only two years before Mahler wrote his symphony.
He must have felt the terror of the reports.
He probably even talked to Caruso about it.

What might Mahler
Have thought of California?
When he saw Niagara Falls he said,
"At last, *fortissimo!*"
What if Mahler had lived
Through the earthquake?
Would he still have written
*Das Lied von der Erde*
About a place of such hedonistic
Pleasure and reflection?

The songs are all about sex that
People did not have but wanted to.
Yet in the *Abschied*, an oboe and harp
Murmur beautifully about how peaceful
And calm the world is. But it is not.
Only in art and music is the world calm
And peaceful, and we must always be sure
That we are not telling lies to ourselves,
At least not lies that might hurt.

The actual song of the earth is violent
And painful and has absolutely no idea
We are here. That is the brilliant sadness
Of Mahler: he knows that.

He knows that the earth
Would be infinitely happier
If we were not here at all.
It was perfectly fine in the millions
Of years between the dinosaurs and us.
The time when the earth just enjoyed itself.

Mahler tries to find the reason we are here.
But you can tell he secretly knows:
There is no reason.
And there does not need to be a reason.
There is no need for us to be here,
Except to notice that we are here at all
And to be grateful for the noticing.
Just notice. Just listen.

It is challenging not to think that
*Das Lied von der Erde* is
Not at all about the earth
And is just about Mahler
And the greatest thing about it,
Is that it is so beautiful.
And it is too much,
And it is enough,
That it is all about him.
He was enough.
Ever. Ever. Ever. Ever.
And because he noticed,
We are enough, too.

# Patty, Sally, Phyllis

The Washington girls.
They are all gone now.
The first three singers
I ever knew who could
Really sing like stars.

No, they were not *like* stars.
They were stars. It is just that
No one outside of Washington
Really knew them. But I did.

And my life would never
Have happened had I not.

They were, for a short time,
One woman in three.
Sally jealous of Phyllis.
Patty worrying about nine children.
Phyllis trying in vain to get her husband to love her.

All three had awful husbands.
All three had major voices.
"Major," as we call them
In my business. Silly words.

They were my first divas.
And how I loved them.
Sally was the most complex.
A large family,
A radiant light within her,

And dark screaming demons within
Who could never quite overtake her
But they plagued her every hour.

Patty lived simply and did not
Think heavily or deeply about life.
She lived, loved, and coped.
She was happy, probably for most
Of every single day of her long life.
She lived the longest.

When I went to visit Phyllis
In her final days, she was in a bed
In the place where Sally used to work.
Her life was slowly ebbing away,
Possessed by a monster that killed her,
A monster that would momentarily allow
Her to surface and speak to me, and when
She did, it was absolutely her for a second,
Then the monster would scream back and grab.

She knew it was me, then she didn't.
"We did whatever we wanted, didn't we?
We didn't care one bit what anybody said!"
People thought it was odd, me a teenager,
Phyllis in her late forties, probably, by then.
We were Harold and Maude, the best of friends.

It was Phyllis I turned to for everything.
She was a parent to me, in a way she probably
Never could be for her own children.
I told her, with great fear and tears,
As we stood on the banks of the Wabash

In Vincennes, right at the George Rogers Clark,
That I thought I knew that I was gay, and if I was,
What was my life going to be like?

"The people who really love you will love you,
No matter who you are. And the people who can't
Love you won't love you no matter what you do."
In those few words, she taught me how to live,
How not to waste time on people who cannot love.
She spoke from the bitterest experience, as she spent
Her life chasing a man who just could not love her
In a way that she could feel as love.

Even worse, he could not hear her voice.
And of all of my first three divas,
Hers was the voice. They were all wonderful,
But Phyllis had a unique talent, one I have seen
Many times over since I met her, and many have
Been just as sad, under-sung, and unheard.

Since she died, she came to me in the
　dreamscape, she asked me to take
Her urn out of where she is, next to her husband,
And spread the ashes on the banks of the Wabash.

Is she is actually visiting?
Or am I just remembering a twilight conversation
That meant the entire world to me, when my own
Voice was first heard?
I miss my old singing girls.

# Chipmunk

During that long pandemic summer,
I drove to Indiana, afraid I may never
See my family again. No one knew.
It was the dead time of 2020.
I was given a house in Bloomington,
Halfway between my brothers.

The house of many colors.
Each wall of the house is different.
Very unconventional for Indiana.
But a really sweet and fun house.
"I'm building that bridge for him"
Is in the dining room.

I went to stay for two weeks.
Then a huge outbreak of Covid
At home, so I decided to stay,
For one month, then two.
In truth, I did not want to go home.
I was unhappy there, and refused facts.

Every night, the huge campus was empty.
I would walk all over it,
Traversing the paths I trod
Thirty and forty years ago, some of it
Even fifty years ago, when all of my
Dreams were big ones, but it was not
A place where I ever imagined I could go.

There is the place I first listened to Wagner.

And the dorm where I first heard *Sweeney Todd*.
And where I saw Vladimir Horowitz,
And Leontyne Price.

I walked by all of my old dorm rooms.
Where I first and last kissed Kevin,
Where I wished for more than I had.
Where my parents waited for me to
Take me home and hear about my dreams.

Then one night, near the end of the trip,
There was a dead deer in someone's yard.
He looked huge. And the stench was terrible.
The deer had taken over the town, and we all
Saw them everywhere, so the loss was worse.

Just today, in Aspen, I swerved to miss a
Chipmunk in the road, but I hit him.
He was suffering terribly, not yet dead.
There was no saving him.
Birds were hovering to eat him
Even as I turned the car around.

I had to be merciful
And run over him again.
He must have seen my
Enormous vehicle
Coming towards him
Just before his life ended.

I had no choice.
I could not let him suffer.
At the moment I did it.
I thought of that huge deer

And the little chipmunk.
And I wept for an hour.

# First World Problem

My Aspen condo.
Yes, I know.
People who have condos
In Aspen do not write poems
And naturally do not write poems
About problems in their condo.

It is a beautiful place.
It is not mine.
I just stay here.
But it is home, too.

There is one bathroom.
Upstairs near the door.
That looks like snakeskin.
And I am terrified to go in.

Because I am always so sure
That I will find a snake in there.
And then I will have to move out.
Or I would have to call the office
And be very embarrassed to say
That I found a snake and could
They please come and remove it
But do not kill it because I could not.

So I do not go in that bathroom
Because I am always sure
There is a snake in there.
Are our minds really like that?

# Carrying the Mountains Home

## Eight short prose poems of farewell for the Aspen Opera Theater and Vocal Arts Artists of 2023

**ONE**

There is a forever time,
Hours before the sun,
When the pulse
Of the wakening world,
Those welcoming winds,
Perform their radical
Quotidian miracle.

This is the great creative holiness
Which nature confers on us.
Some old gods are here still: Janus,
Julius, Augustus, remain to name our months.

Preserving care, and
Ancestral legacies;
That is our wish for you
To carry from these mountains.

In the shadows over there,
Can you see them?
Ancestors are here.
Yours. Mine.
They stand sentinel.

Mozart is here, too,
Hovering in the aspens,
Giggling with each flutter.
He sings to the bears
And calms the nervous deer.

**TWO**

I will remember the faces of this summer,
And most especially the radiant voices
Who vibrated this thin air with joy and aspiration.
We will all remember your fears and awakenings,
Your wows and confusions,
Your tears and smiles,
Which cannot exist without each other.

We are all divided selves,
Guessing at associations,
Trying on the clothes of others
To await what fits,
Until we do not.

Singing is the thing
That leads to the
Deeper thing
Without which
No other things matter.

**THREE**

Seventy-five million summers ago,
The *Tyrannosaurus rex*
Drank from Castle Creek.
Back when dinosaurs
Echoed through this very valley,

A tiny atomic part of each of us
Was already here.

It must amaze us, always,
That Castle Creek flows
To the Roaring Fork
And then on to the Colorado.
The water we have heard and seen
Each day flows, eventually,
Through the Grand Canyon,
Yearning to find its ocean.

What survives
From those
Unimaginable eons,
From those moments
Depicted just days ago
With such beauty in
John Luther Adams's *Atlas*?

What is still here,
Outside of our obvious
Evolving necessities?

One survivor,
A thing we have
That dinosaurs had,
That all primates still share,
Is the ear, our oldest ancestor.

**FOUR**

In utero, we have the power
To hear, to touch, to see.

But we have no need of it,
Since all needs are met.

Then suddenly, like the great C major
Of the Haydn *Creation*,
The light awakens,
The wakening world ignites.
(Surely, the greatest C major in music.)

In an instant,
All of our senses activate,
And we know exactly what to do,
Though we cannot know what help we need.
Forgive yourself for not knowing something.

**FIVE**

Artistry is a fullness
That demands emptiness.
It staves off limitations,
It seeks nourishment as
It opens other amazements:
That we are under a sky,
That trees reach for the same light
That we accept as ours.

Opera, with only 423 birthdays,
Begs us, constantly, clearly,
Maddeningly, expensively, cheaply,
Just to be itself, to let it sing.
It longs for our accomplishment.

Remember a few precious things,
If not now, later:

The industry is not the art,
But what gives you industry
Cannot be anything *but* art.

You will, one day soon,
Have a day that will
Be fully yours, a shifted *you*.
You will walk into a room
And not think, "I wonder what
They all think of me?"
Instead, you will think,
"I wonder what I
Think of all of them?"

## SIX

Our task in art is to *really* hear
The inner voice which is ours alone.
We must shut down those nervous,
Terrified, sad, doubting selves,
All of those other clever pretenders
Who think they are you or me,
And who fight with the real.

## SEVEN

Lift, please,
This always-lumbering art,
Which is not dying,
But is constantly wheezing.
We check its vital signs every day.

Art needs you to
Raise it where it droops.
Make the old world new,

And give the new world a taste
Of the beauty for which it longs.

Be artistic citizens worth fighting for.
Spend outrage only on the outrageous.
Spend love on everything else.
Changing your mind, after all,
Is proof you have one.

## EIGHT

Leave this August sky towards another,
With your ear turned towards yourself.
You are an ancestor, too,
Who lives on in this valley,
Amidst the dancing trees,
Down the creek,
Towards the great ocean.

# New York City, Autumn 2022

The city of dreams,
And so many broken ones.
Decay and decrepitude mixed
With the best of everything.
The center of the world.

When we were children,
NYC was the center of the 1970s.
And for us, this is always our NYC:
*Marathon Man, Annie Hall, Taxi Driver
Saturday Night Fever, Dog Day Afternoon
Midnight Cowboy*, the Pinto Inline font of
The poster of *A Chorus Line*.

The credit sequences of *The Jeffersons*
And *All in the Family*, that smoky and unclear
Helicopter shot of New York, are what we all thought
NYC was going to be when we ever managed
To get there.

Worst weekend in New York ever,
The one that should have been the best:
We went to a gorgeous wedding, my spouse and I.
The entire time he was texting with his new guy.
The romantic time that should have been ours
Was handed to another person, someone who
Had invested nothing in him, someone with
Nothing at all to lose. One of life's takers.

It bothered neither of them, not even an iota,
What they had taken from me, nor what pain
I was in from their cruel actions.
They simply did not care.
They still don't.

That became New York for me.
For a very long time.
But eventually, New York became
Walks in Soho again. Those trendy and
Heavenly shops below Houston Street.
It became the nights after the theater,
Descending into the darker streets after
An amazing play. I remember leaving
*All My Sons.* John Lithgow. Diane Wiest.
Patrick Wilson. And years before, leaving
*Lettuce and Lovage* for the third night
In a row. Maggie Smith. Margaret Tyzack.
Each performance slightly different.

New York always comes back,
Each time slightly different.
There was an apartment building
45th and 8th, called Camelot, or it was then.
I dated a guy who lived there and I thought
He was the greatest guy ever, the forever one.
I fell so hard for him, probably harder than for
Anyone except for Paul in Australia.
There is a pattern here: fall hard and ignore
All of the signs that he is not a good idea.
I even obsessed over another man in Oz
Just to distract myself from Paul.
Set myself aside, time after time,
For the wrong guy.

So many times, arriving in New York.
I would be driven across the Triborough
And decide that if I saw a train,
That would be my best omen for
How the trip would be.

And the omen has always been true.
When I see a train, the trip is a good one.

# Marfa

One cannot see Marfa.
It is a phenomenon
Maybe not only of the Permian Basin
That you cannot see it.
You will be driving along,
And a glorious vista will appear.
Then, suddenly, it is gone.

From Alpine to Fort Davis,
There are incredible peaks
Off to the left, especially.
But then they disappear.
It is an ancient sea.
And it can feel like
You are still underwater.

The skies are so glorious.
The utter quiet.
What did it sound like
During the receding of
The great ocean and the
Rifts and events that made
These mountains?

To stand in Marfa and see
The distant waves frozen
Between me and the sunset
Is to see all of time.

We are always able to see

Millions of everything
If that is what we choose.
Often we only look at the new.

The art at Marfa is all new.
It talks to the old just as clearly
As that ancient ocean speaks to
Us these 450 million years later.

"Why?" it seems to ask us,
Do you worry about silly things,
And loves that did not come to you,
When you have this majestic old world?

# Untitled (dawn to dusk)
## Marfa, Texas

Light and dark by half.
Halves speaking by quarters.
Light dancing slowly on
Translucent ghosts.

The knowing and observing selves,
Walking through the black and white
Beauty, sitting like memories they live
Each day in our most silent places.

It is a place we never wish to leave
Because to see it in all times of day.
Would we begin to see ourselves,
For there is nothing but ourselves,
If we live in its absolute beauty?

A liminal building
A nodal point of all
We are, in any moment
Within dawn to dusk,
In a space of reflection and repose,
living with us like friends.

# Swimming Under the Blue Moon

The scorching hill country
Beautiful, dry, struggling to survive,
So little water for the earth's demands.

So one feels guilt in Marfa or gorgeous
Old Fredericksburg when swimming
In a beautiful pool under a blue moon.

In Marfa the pool is a roofless church
Framing the pewter sky with moonbeams.

In the hill country, there is no frame,
No walls, no church around the pool.
It is all God, open to the firmament.

Wasps and bees use the pool,
So it is not all luxury.
Their needs are Spartan.

Swimming under the blue super moon
One of the most ravishing sights ever,
A cardinal finished his day poolside,
As if trying to tell me something.

From nowhere, an enormous wind
Blew up the *hügel*, as the old settlers
Would have called this place.

It was violent and huge, blowing water
From the pool and moving tables and chairs.
The cardinal never moved from his spot,
Looking directly at me.

The rare moon, the cardinal, and the wind.
Will my mind ever be quiet enough
For me to begin to understand
What was I being told?

# Sunset in China

Leaving the old Shanghai Conservatory,
The last time I saw it, in the early 1990s,
I noticed a strangely orange sunset.

From this sky would leaders of China
Look west and dream about their country?
The setting sun at the moment was lighting
Europe's morning, and would then roll across
The ocean and to my homeland.

It was the farthest from home I ever was,
And I did not realize what that would mean.
I spent so many lonely nights in China,
Exhausted from the endless days of work.

The work never ended. Their needs were great.
All of them searching for a voice.
The endless bottomless cups of tea.
The thin cigarettes that tasted of nothing.

We wondered about our small moment
About our difficult rehearsals.
The singers arriving on bicycles.
Riding off into the night in their tuxes.

Were we giving them glimpses of lives
They could not sustain in their country?
Would they be allowed to study abroad?
And what would they do if they could not?

I felt enormous responsibility but held
Very little power over them besides the
Energy I could give to music, so I gave it all.
I sang all day, every day, to get them to imitate.
Get them to make any kind of sound resembling
Opera, the thing they most sought from me.

Opera, the great imperial remnant.
The begetter of souls, the attainment,
The Mozart aria that gives you a voice
Where all others are silent.

That which gives us voice
Is as necessary to the world
As the golden sunset that
Beckoned me west from a world
In which I was a distant sad visitor.

# September

We are the many things we love.
But we must always also love
Walking away from that which
Is not meant for us to love.

Sometimes people walk into your life
And you are reminded why it never
Worked with someone you thought
You would love until the end of time.

We all have so many ghosts
Of old pains and words we
Should have spoken on the right day.
And when you should have bolted.

If you feel you are hard to love,
Walk away from whoever made
You feel anything even close to that.
I wish I could forget you as easily
As you forgot about me.
How a person acts is your answer
To every question. Hear them.

Neither you nor I nor anyone
Will ever change anything
By loving it harder.
If you have been wounded
But are still kind to others,
You are a gift to the world.

The right person will choose you.
Do not force or press anyone.
What stays is what is supposed to stay.
Do not be afraid of anger, for anger
Is the bridge to life's next stage.

There is pain in these poems.
But huge joy as well.
Each word has kissed my soul
With sorrow's ironic gentleness.
One cannot love someone so much
That you do the loving for both of you.
Poems are armor.
They sit in that intricate place
Where the world's image
Feels the September air.
September, the month of forgiveness.

I am many people.
To some I am talented.
To some I am a hack.
To some I am a discovery.
To some I am the oldest news.
To him, I am all angry distance.
To me, I had to save myself
From more wracking pain
And endless chaotic anxiety.
Who am I, though, to me?

Please, may I ask one thing?
Take this moment, this single moment
Of reading this short simple sentence.
Use it to remember that you are safe,
And remember one sunset.

Remember what no one should ever forget.
For who will remember, if not you?
Remember this single moment with joy.
Remember the gift of this small time.

# A Poem for Lynn Wyatt
## Opening of Lynn Wyatt Square for the Performing Arts
## September 21, 2023

Once a letter reached her from France.
It was addressed, simply,
Lynn Wyatt, Texas.

She is poetry and prose.
So sometimes she rhymes.
So well she chose,
To read between lines.

Inspired by her favorite Grace,
The famous Princess of Monaco,
Her neighbor of many years.
She is that same foreverland
Of kindness and grace,
A world not ours yet she makes it ours.
Her greatest gifts are her time,
her advocacy, and her love.
She has an orbit,
Because she is a sun,
A center of gravity.
When she is your friend,
You really have really known a friend.

Grace is a word without synonym or cynicism.
Grace describes this beautiful newly gifted space,
This gathering place for a great city.

When Lynn says the arts are a city's soul,
She means it.

A moment of reflection on those who
Give of themselves for no other reason
Than to make life better for others.
How miraculous they are.
How rare. How needed.
How Lynn.
How grateful we are.

Art tells the truth when life cannot.
Art is not just distraction from our
Sometimes joylessly hectic hours.
Art is fundamental. She understands this.
Artists are souls searching for meaning.
She also understands this.

Only one thing will complete this square,
And bring Lynn all of her future joy.
The artists from the great companies
You can see from this very spot,
They are this square. They will fill it.
And most especially, the audiences who will
Gather here before and after events
That will define their memories.
They will bring the most joy to Lynn,
And bring her family pride in what she gave here.

When great symphonies play,
When Shakespeare speaks,
When Tchaikovsky's Clara soars,
And when the world's

Great singers vibrate our air,
They will gather here
For generations to come.

And when they do,
They will remember the
People who change the world
Just by walking into a room.
They will remember Lynn,
And her perfect sense of occasion,
Giving so generously
Of her own blessings.

They will remember the Lynn
We all know and love today.
The Lynn of laughter and smiles,
The Lynn who gets things done.
She's Gucci and Verdi,
La Mauresque to *La Bohème*,
Chanel, Tasajillo, and Beethoven.
Neil Simon and Chekhov.
Great soufflés and nutcrackers.

All over the world
We have been together, dear Lynn,
Enjoying the shared joys of people.
Now, that joy will gather here
In this place you have made.

Ancestors gather,
Silently watching us now.
Half a mile from here,
at Allen's Landing,
Houston began.

Who would have imagined
That 187 years later
A square would rise with such beauty?
We can almost hear old Sam Houston
Cursing through laughter
At the absurdity of it all,
Sounding perhaps a bit like Oscar
At his salty best, and
Loving it all the while.

Yes, sometimes she rhymes,
As so will the end of this poem.

Lady Gaga quipped
With a knowing grin,
That if she grew up,
She'd want to be Lynn.

Looking dazzling always,
Even awful magenta.
Lynn treasures three Oscars:
Her own, Elton's party, and then de la Renta.

For all of her glamor,
She's not highfalutin'
So we cut her some slack
For that room: Helmut Newton.

Never explain.
Never complain.
Do nothing mundane
With Shirley MacLaine.
Just remember the ice cube
For Lynn's champagne.

Thank you, dear Lynn
For this peerless occasion
The city can now have
A beautiful invasion.

Of grateful Houstonians
Enjoying their art,
And realizing, always,
That they live in a place
Of such overwhelming
Generosity, grace, and style.

We are proud to be today
Where that letter once found you:
Lynn Wyatt, Texas.

# The Prison of Time

To wake with a person,
Having exhausted our desires
For hours in the night before,
The need still sitting on our skin,
Is to feel time's endless prison.

Knowing that some hearts only
Understand each other in silence,
In the accepted touch that travels
Like a tributary to love's ocean.

Loving this touch tells us who we are,
So why does the promise of more time
Fill me with such endless burdensome agony?
Am I in fear that I will miss something else?
Or am I afraid that I will not feel more
Of what I love more than anything to feel?

When we look back on time wasted,
What is it we are mourning?
We cannot have that time returned to us.
The endless lonely hours in Bregenz,
When I was on the floor crying in such
Palpable agony that a doctor reported that
I had been physically attacked, why did I
Continue to sit in the prison of that time?

This is what we do.
We construct our own prisons.
Then we hold on to them

Because of course they feel safe,
Since we designed them for ourselves.
We do not learn to love the sound
Of our own feet walking away
From that which can harm us.

A photograph will imprison time forever,
Freezing a moment and the smell and feel.
But we look at images constantly,
Never thinking of most of them again.
Then that one photo comes along,
That one look into a person's eyes
And a prison emerges.

There can be no thoughtless *we*.
Not in these remaining precious days.
Forgive yourself for liberation from
The prisons you so happily built.
Let the sun rise again on the hills
You forgot to climb and the rosemary
And thyme and tuberoses you failed
To notice during years of captivity.

Can I be kinder to everyone,
Most especially to myself?
Can I soften my gaze at the world
As I slowly liberate each moment
From the bonds
Of warm and old longings,
Learned so well and for so long
From loving unknowingness?

www.ingramcontent.com/pod-product-compliance
Lightning Source LLC
Chambersburg PA
CBHW051342040426
42453CB00007B/370